Fly With Me

Walter W. Gowing

*To MacKenzie,
Some highlights of my days with Pan American World Airways. The best service carved by course meal service — on the Boeing stratocruiser. Then the jet in 1960. Great crews & passengers.
Jean Foyle*

WaltStar Publishing Company

Copyright © 2016 Walter W. Gowing

Cover illustration © Walter W. Gowing

Cover, graphic and text design by Stephanie Rogers

ISBN: 1533179123
ISBN-13: 978-1533179128

All rights reserved. No part of this book may be reproduced in any form or by any electronic or mechanical means, including information storage and retrieval systems, without prior permission from the copyright owner, except by a reviewer who may quote brief passages in a review.

WaltStar Publishing Company
Penthouse 8
237 King Street West
Cambridge, Ontario, Canada
N3H 5L2

For my wife of 63 years, Lillian Joyce Gowing.

BOOKS BY WALTER W. GOWING

Tender Roots

I was there

Orange Juice In My Fountain Pen

Fly With Me

ACKNOWLEDGMENTS

Behind the scenes there are many people who help to transport an author's idea from its beginnings to the finished product of the published book you are holding in your hands. I want to acknowledge some of these key people who have assisted me in the process.

Thank you to Veronica Kerr, a travel specialist at Bullas Travel in Kitchener, Ontario who arranged to get me in and out of many exotic places in this world.

Betty King, a life-long friend, who is my best critic and an advisor in reading my early manuscripts. Betty is a former teacher-librarian.

Rob Bullas, president of Bullas Travel, is a friend who has accompanied me on some exciting adventures. Not surprisingly, he is the subject of several stories in this book.

Jean Fayle, a delightful person who took the time to allow me to interview her on many occasions. First, for a newspaper story that intrigued me so much that I went back for more information. It is a vital part of the formula to this book.

I thank Stephanie Rogers, my granddaughter and an accomplished sports writer and graphic designer who worked for such papers as the Miami Herald. Her computer wizardry and ingenious suggestions are greatly appreciated.

There is one other person who has the most influence on my writing and my life. That, of course is my wife Lillian, who is also my personal editor and best friend. These stories wouldn't be possible without her allowing me to drag her to all four corners of the world.

I give my sincerest thanks and gratitude to all of these people in my latest endeavor to publish this book.

WALTER W. GOWING

CONTENTS

PART ONE

FLIGHTLESS BIRDS

Chapter 1: Happy Harry	1
Chapter 2: Fairy Penguins	21
Chapter 3: On The Rocks	27
Chapter 4: Big Bird	33

PART TWO

PLANES AND TRAINS

Chapter 5: Cold, Cold, Cold	49
Chapter 6: Puffing Billy	57
Chapter 7: The Big Drip	63
Chapter 8: The Next Seat	81

PART THREE

THE OUTBACK

Chapter 9: Ghost Towns	93
Chapter 10: Train Wreck	105
Chapter 11: Oh, Those Swinging Doors!	111

PART FOUR

PAN AM GIRL

Chapter 12: Just Jean	127
Chapter 13: "Sierra Pappa!"	141
Chapter 14: Oops, Sorry Mr. Kennedy!	153
Chapter 15: The Opium Den	161
Chapter 16: In Love	169

PART FIVE

DOWN UNDER

Chapter 17: Dinner is Served	179
Chapter 18: The Lost Glacier	183
Chapter 19: Welcome, Prime Minister	187
Chapter 20: Recipe Swap	199
Chapter 21: The Chef	205
Afterword	215
The Author	217

PART ONE

FLIGHTLESS BIRDS

CHAPTER 1

HAPPY HARRY

The little fellow tilted his head to the right and with a smile that only a penguin can express, looked up at me and captured my heart. Who said penguins can't smile?

There I was, standing alone with nearly a million of the most loveable of God's creatures, on a windswept, near-barren piece of land scattered with a few scrubby bushes. I was in the region of Patagonia; that cruel, desolate stretch of land in the southern part of Argentina. This dry, uninviting plateau covers nearly one quarter of Argentina's 2,780,400 square kilometre (1,073,500 square mile) land mass.

This is a tantalizing tale. Come along and "Fly With Me." My wife Lillian and I flew out of Canada's busiest airport, Toronto's Pearson International Airport on a small plane to Atlanta, Georgia. Once there, we boarded a Delta Airlines Boeing 767 to Buenos Aires, Argentina. It almost seems ironic that when we left Toronto it was pouring rain. I mean buckets of water coming down from the heavens. As I stood on that dry, parched desert land of Patagonia where rain is rarely seen, I wondered how we could move the abundance of water from Canada to this shriveled up land in South America.

After a day in Buenos Aires, we boarded a plane to Iguacu Falls on Argentina's northern border with Brazil. Crossing into Brazil by car, we spent several exciting days exploring the Iguacu River and its 275 waterfalls. This was an unbelievable sight of unique water power crashing down some 72 metres (237 feet) to continue its journey across the country. Compare this to Canada's Horseshoe Falls at Niagara Falls, Ontario, where the drop is only 51 metres (167 feet) with a width of 792 metres (2,600 feet). Iguacu Falls extends some three kilometres (two miles) of waters cascading over the brink.

While exploring lands near the falls, Lillian and I saw some green iguanas. These pre-historic looking creatures can grow to about 1.8 metres (six feet) in length, though the ones we found in the trees were about half that size. We came across many white egrets, and butterflies by the thousands. The brown Capuchin monkeys are plentiful, but sometimes are a real nuisance. There were quite a few broad-snout Caimans in the jungle; they belong to the alligator family.

Lillian and I have been to Victoria Falls, an impressive sight that straddles the border between Zambia and Zimbabwe in Africa. By contrast, Victoria Falls is twice the height of Niagara Falls. We were above the falls on a small flat-bottom boat with a diesel engine. It is a little nerve-wracking if you think that the engine might quit, because the alternatives include going over the falls, being plundered by a hippopotamus, or being eaten by a crocodile.

In Patagonia, I wondered again if it would be possible to divert some of that water from the Iguacu River south to the dry lands. Maybe a pipeline could take the water south?

After our flight back from the adventurous wilds of Iguacu to the friendly hospitality of Buenos Aires, we took time to enjoy its great nightlife and its tango clubs. We took a few days to explore and enjoy the city and some of the rural areas that surround the metropolis and its three million people.

Get that right foot up behind your left leg and raise your right knee while swinging your partner around to that mesmerizing music. Hey, I'm doing the tango! This syncopated ballroom dance music originated in Argentina. It was fascinating to watch some of the dancers perform these intricate steps, whether it be on the dance hall floor or on the streets of the city.

Shopping was marvelous in the centre of the city. We had hired a driver to escort us around during our visit. At one shop, I purchased two pairs of pants and a couple of beautiful white shirts with a little blue trim and button-down collars. The following day, I returned to pick up the pants as the store offered to shorten them for me. I decided to try on the pants again, just to make sure everything fit properly. The first pair was perfect. The second pair, well, something was wrong. I would say very, very wrong. They had shortened one leg twice and it was halfway up to my knee, while they'd forgotten to shorten the other leg at all. The second pant leg was about a foot too long.

When I bought the clothes the day before, our guide and interpreter Lorena was with us. Today, I was in the store on my own. The store employees spoke only Spanish and I had only English to offer in return. It was back to that universal sign language. I've relied on it in China, Malaysia, and many other countries to communicate when there was a language barrier. The clerks soon realized the problem and got another pair of pants off the rack. One pointed to the clock to indicate that in 30 minutes they would be shortened and ready to pick up. That was fine by me. The second time around, the pants fit perfectly, and by all counts the legs were the same length.

It was time to leave our boutique hotel in this exciting South American city with its streets filled with people rushing about, circling around the tango dancers and the artists selling their amazing brightly-coloured paintings. On almost every busy pedestrian street, no automobiles are allowed. There were pretty, scantily-clad girls in costume, coaxing male passersby to have their picture taken with them, for a fee of course.

We made our way to the harbor to catch a ship south to the town of Puerto Madryn. It is neatly tucked into the back of a sheltered bay called Golfo Nuevo. Across the bay is Puerto Piramides, very close to the lowest piece of land in South America. It is 40 metres (131 feet) below sea level. Lillian and I have been to the Dead Sea, shared by Israel and Jordan, where the land drops to 424 metres (1,391 feet) below sea level. It's the lowest place in the world.

After leaving Buenos Aires, we crossed the infamous River Plate to make a stop at Montevideo, Uruguay. There we saw the Graf Spee monument, including the anchor of the German battleship that was scuttled in the mouth of the River Plate, just outside Montevideo Bay at the beginning of the Second World War.

In the fall of 1939, the Graf Spee became notorious for the sinking of nine British merchant ships. Shortly after, three British warships, the cruiser Exeter, and the light cruisers Ajax and Achilles, attacked the German pocket battleship, greatly damaging it on the River Plate. The Graf Spee made a run for it to the neutral port of Montevideo, where it spent only a few days. There wasn't enough time for it to be fully repaired and it wasn't ready for another battle with its enemies.

The commander of the Graf Spee, Captain Hans Langsdorff, knew the British were waiting for it if it left the River Plate and headed into international waters. The

German captain did not want the British to capture the prized ship, so he scuttled the ship, sending it to the bottom of the river. A few days later, Captain Langsdorff committed suicide rather than being captured by the British navy.

Lillian and I were in Mexico City shortly after the release of the British film *The Battle of the River Plate* in 1956. The film starred John Gregson, Anthony Quayle and Peter Finch. The lengthy film ran well over two hours, and the theatre had three intermissions during the show. It turned out we had some great conversations with the man sitting next to us that night.

He was a lieutenant-inspector in the Mexico City police department and was attending the screening to help improve his English. Our conversations with him helped his cause, and the information about his city helped us to learn more about life in Mexico. He offered to show us around the city over the next few days and this was a great experience. We toured in his open convertible with special privileges wherever we went, due to his high ranking in the police force.

How memories flow back when current experiences excite the mind. It was an interesting string of trips from Toronto to Puerto Madryn, via Buenos Aires, Iguacu and Montevideo. Once we disembarked the ship, I was prepared for an early morning trip south to visit the Punta Tombo Rookery and its one million inhabitants. We were warned that it would be a dusty, dirty and rough venture on transportation equipment that was ready for the scrap heap many years ago. We had been on the go for several days, and Lillian wisely decided to stay in Puerto Madryn and wait for my return.

It was like sounding the battle cry when climbing aboard a World War One army tank and charging over the rough terrain as if we were going into war. I climbed into an old yellow school bus that had more dents in it than a tin can used by a group of kids playing kick-the-can. It was a retired school bus from North America that had long ago seen its better days. Several of the windows were missing and in more than one place there were holes in the floor. As we traveled along, you could look through the floor and see the paved road below. We travelled for some time when we made a stop at the town of Trelew for some refreshments. I think the real reason for the stop was to refresh this old clunker that we were riding in. I noticed the driver adding some oil to the engine and some water to the radiator. Back on the bus, by this time referred to as the "junk dealer's special," we made a sharp turn off the paved highway and headed farther south on a dusty unpaved road. It was more like a camel trail in the desert.

It was hot and a bit windy that day. We were blessed by the fact that this was a lonely stretch of road not far from the Atlantic coast and with very little traffic. Every so often there was the odd vehicle, usually an old relic in the form of a pickup truck or sometimes a small stake truck that would pass us. I always carry a handkerchief in my pocket and thank goodness I had it on this occasion. Each time something passed us in a cloud of dust, I would reach for my handkerchief to cover my face. There were only about half a dozen people on the bus and everyone was coughing and choking each time the dust blew into the bus. The dust from the motor vehicles passing us flowed into the bus through the spaces of missing windows and holes in the floor. Honestly, the driver couldn't see at times. He sometimes slowed down to almost a stop, but then when you think about it, he wasn't traveling all that fast to start with, driving that rickety old piece of scrap from Canada or the U.S. I often found myself staring through one of the holes in the bus floor, watching the reddish dry earth pass by below. There is iron in the soil in this area of Patagonia and the earth reflects this in its sometimes orange or reddish colour.

Finally, after more than 160 kilometres (100 miles) and several hours of ungodly red dust from the road, we arrived at Punta Tombo. I would hate to make this trip in the wrong season of the year when the penguins have travelled north in the Atlantic waters to Uruguay and Brazil. After stumbling off the bus and making my way across the barren country on foot, I saw the penguins.

Now I'm about 1,600 kilometres (1,000 miles) south of Buenos Aires in a desolate part of Patagonia where there are no stores, no people and no gas stations, just penguins for as far as I could see. Being in the midst of a flock of these flightless birds did remind me a bit of being in the midst of a herd of cattle on the ranch where we had spent some time near Buenos Aires. It was there that I rode horseback with the gauchos, rounding up horses and cattle. Gauchos are free-spirited South American cowboys. Gauchos have inspired the arts in Argentina through stories, books, paintings and music. In the early days, they lived a lonely life out on the Pampas. Today, the large ranches of the Pampas raise thousands of head of cattle. The gauchos are vital to the success of the industry. Argentinian beef is shipped around the world.

I wasn't alone on this adventure of Wild West living on the Pampas. My sidekick, cowgirl Lillian, helped me drive the chuck wagon that carried the supplies. Gauchos are pretty hefty eaters after an all-day ride on horseback. Sitting around a roaring fire at night and eating off a tin plate under the stars set a great atmosphere for the exaggerated stories gauchos like to tell of the exciting wild past on the Pampas. Stories were told of gauchos roaming the Pampas back in the 1600's. In those days they were called mestizos. They owned only the clothes they wore and the horse they rode. Well, one can even question the ownership of the horse, as it was usually a stolen animal.

It was only a matter of days from that Pampas experience with the gauchos to this lonely, remote location in southern Argentina where there were no people, only penguins. Back on the ranch, the casual dress code was much different than here on the Punta Tombo Nature Reserve.

For the penguins a tuxedo is the dress code of the day at Punta Tombo. I was surprised how easy it was to walk around amongst the formally-dressed birds. There they were, outfitted in black from the top of their heads all the way down their backs to the tip of their stubby tails. Their sleek front was like a perfectly starched white shirt. There was a white ring circling their neck and running over their heads, ending at their black beak. They were dressed for a Broadway musical.

They all looked the same to me and I'm told they look the same to one another. It's by their voice that they're known. You know who your partner is by the sounds they make. When penguin parents return from a fishing expedition with food for dinner, the young penguins call out to mom and dad so they know where to find them. They all sounded the same to me, but of course I'm a human and not privy to their dialect. It is a bit of a braying noise that could compare to a donkey's sound, but without a doubt, these little creatures standing straight up on their two webbed feet are birds. Encountering a flock of penguins is much like being surrounded by a flock of sheep or a herd of goats. I was once in New Zealand in the centre of a flock of sheep 4,000 animals deep. They stampeded, but I stood still and they went around me. Not a single one touched me. It was a safe escape.

Here at the reserve, I am in the midst of penguins at one of the largest rookeries in the world, isolated from most human beings and protected by the Government of Argentina. This is home to the Magellanic penguin from at least September each year until the following April. They take over the territory, laying eggs and hatching their young. About 50 percent of the chicks die of hunger and thirst before it is time to move north up the Atlantic coast.

As I stood there marveling at these little "people" surrounding me, they went about their activities just as if I didn't exist. That is, all except one little tyke. He edged right up to me, crowding against my left leg and nestling his head into my thigh. It was like I was his long-lost cousin.

I took one step sideways and looked down at the little fellow. He shuffled three or four times in the same direction and was tight up against me again. There we were, standing tight against one another in the middle of a million penguins. I looked down at the remarkable little creature, my heart fluttered, and a tear came into my eye when I said, "Hello, Harry."

I don't know why I called him Harry. I guess he just looked like a Harry to me. He was sweet, adorable, and I was his best friend.

Harry was at home in Patagonia, a land scientists say

hasn't changed in 45 million years. My Magellanic friend is from the family of Spheniscus magellanicus, which sounds pretty impressive to me. The Magellanic name is credited to the Portuguese explorer Ferdinand Magellan, who first witnessed these flightless birds in 1520.

The Magellanic penguins are somewhat like many humans who have a winter home and a summer place. Canadians often spent their summers, however short they might be, enjoying time at home. When the unpleasantries of winter strike, they find refuge in the warm weather of Florida or the Caribbean. You must remember that Argentina is south of the equator and the seasons are opposite to those north of that magical line that runs around the middle of our planet.

When April rolls around in Patagonia, it's beginning to chill down after a warm summer. The waters flowing up from Antarctica turn the Patagonia coastline into a much colder winter atmosphere and it becomes harder to find the food needed for a million "little people" trying to survive. Both the mature adults and their young are ready to swim north in the Atlantic along the South American coast to the somewhat warmer Uruguay and Brazil. While in Patagonia, the female penguin usually lays two eggs that are jointly cared for by the male and female. The parents must find food in the ocean and bring it back to their young ones until they are old enough to swim and collect food on their own.

What do penguins eat? Well if you had a penguin,

you'd be shopping at the fish market. Their diet consists mostly of fish, squid and crustaceans, which includes shrimp and crabs. Penguins are big eaters for their size. Swimming at fast speeds in the water burns up a lot of energy and requires a lot of food to keep up their strength. That is why they move up and down the eastern coastline of South America as the food supply goes up and down, changing with the currents.

These loveable little creatures do have some enemies. The Magellanic penguins are generally comfortable with their safety on land within their rookery. It is when they hunt for food that danger lurks in ocean waters. The killer whales, seals and sea lions top the list of penguin enemies. The food chain in the ocean is such that the biggest eats the smallest and when these cute little penguins come up against a killer whale, the whale usually wins.

It was nearing the end of February when I visited Harry at his home. It was warm enough to be comfortable when wearing a sweater. After all, I was closer to the Antarctic than I was to the equator. At that moment, it hit me like a block of ice as to why Harry took such a liking to me; I was dressed in long black pants and a long-sleeved sweater that was off-white in colour. I looked like a big penguin.

About 515 kilometres (320 miles) off the southern coast of South America, you'll find the British Falkland

Islands. That's not a long distance for penguins to swim. I have taken pictures of the Falklands and their majestic King penguins. Some stand almost as tall as me. They have a little tinge of red and yellow around their necks and a tuft of red on the back of their heads. Their black back and white fronts give the impression of the penguin wearing a tux – it was easy to see how Harry could have made such a mistake with my identity.

Harry would waddle a short distance away from me and then return to where I was standing. I think he wanted me to follow him. He was heading to the Atlantic shoreline. It was evident he wanted to go in the water and for me to join. He was wearing his all-season suit, good for dry land and wet waters. His webbed feet serve the purpose on land or in the water, too. There was no way I could go into the ocean with my penguin look-alike outfit on. My black shoes may have passed for Harry's feet, but there was no way this get-up was going to jump into the water.

Harry waddled a little closer to the brink of the ocean and turned to look back at me. I waddled a little closer to Harry. Maybe not so much of a waddle, but I shuffled my feet to get closer to my friend. Other penguins were moving in and out of the water. I thought, if only I had brought my bathing suit with me, I could join the group for a dip in the ocean. There were hundreds, thousands of little black and white penguins in sight and not another human soul to be seen. Why did I need a bathing suit? Skinny dipping was an option. Had I lost my senses? Surely sea lions and other predators might be in the water looking for a good meal. I wasn't ready to be served up on a platter just yet.

Harry turned once again and looked at me, and with a call that sounded like the "caw" of a crow, waved a wing that he would be using like a flipper in the water, and took one more step towards the precipice. One leap and Harry was in the air and then in the water. With his wings outstretched like an airplane, he glided through the blue ocean waters. Harry looked like he was flying, darting about and having a wonderful time showing off like a new pilot in a Piper Cub. His movement in the water made me believe he was saying, "Fly with me!" as he soared about the heavenly waters of the South Atlantic. Penguins fly underwater using their flippers that were once wings, the same way birds do in the air.

It was time for me to catch that death-trap transportation contraption once used as a school bus. Waving goodbye to Harry, I hiked back up the slope toward the main gate where I could catch my unconventional ride back to civilization. Once again, I noticed the driver checking the oil and the radiator before letting the hood cover drop with a crashing sound. It wasn't fastened down, so it bounced back up and down the entire trip back to Puerto Madryn. If the choking dust filling the bus, or the shaking and jiggling paired with bouncing on a hard seat didn't keep you awake, it would be the unfastened hood cover. Sleep would be your reward if you survived the long trip back to town.

Not far out of the Punta Tombo Rookery, we encountered a small gambol of guanacos. These gracious-looking animals are sometimes mistaken for llamas. They crossed the dusty road in front of the bus and raced up over a sand dune that separated the sky from the parched roadway. We had just left the ocean's rim teaming with life and an abundance of armadillos, dolphins, sea lions and various rodents who make their homes near the sea, and of course, the Magellanic penguins.

Animals who live along the Patagonian coastline struggle for the very limited food supply on this desert-like landscape. In contrast, those living in the ocean have a seemingly unlimited supply of food as the cold Falkland current sweeps along the dry, arid coast on its way north from Antarctica. The area even attracts whales that find plenty of food for their big appetites. The sea is an underwater garden of food in both plant life and living creatures.

The dry, barren land is opposite to the luxurious ocean. The land makes mother rabbit scrounge all day for food to produce enough milk to feed her young. The Patagonian gray fox hunts the mouse-like opossum that in turn, is foraging for its food among the small lizards, young birds and insects. It is the circle of life in action in this desolate place.

The bus actually came to a near stop when the guanacos crossed our path. They are cousins to camels and look like a smaller version, but without a hump. They loped across the sand with their long necks protruding like submarines' periscopes. They are wool-bearing animals. I had seen these beautiful creatures before in the mountain areas of Peru and Chile. I hadn't expected to see a half dozen guanacos in this part of Patagonia, although nothing should surprise me on this outback trip.

As the bus bumped along, jerking its few passengers from side to side, up and down, there was one other thing that impressed me along this passageway. Local peasants were the main travellers, visiting one another and exchanging produce and handmade goods. It provided them with a link to small villages where they could go to market and to church.

Every so often along the road I would see a small shrine or altar indicating the religious commitment of the local peasant people who created it. On the way down to Punta Tombo, I noticed some of the local people praying at these shrines. Over 90 percent of the people in Argentina are Roman Catholic, however, less than 20 percent of these people are practicing Catholics. About 92 percent of people live in large urban centres like Buenos Aires, with a population of 14 million. The country's total population is about 42 million. In the small towns and villages, religion is the most prevalent. It is the people in these places, who live closest to the earth, who take the time to worship their God. The hectic life of big cities, not only in Argentina but also in many countries of the world, has interfered with religious worship. Along this dusty backcountry road, I found people who put religion first.

The last part of this journey was mostly in the dusk of the evening hours. With dwindling light, we had just noise, dust, and motion. I was glad to finally climb off the dilapidated clunker and reunite with Lillian in Puerto Madryn, eager to share stories for her journal and some fantastic pictures of the penguins.

And just like that, it was time to fly again.

"Chair backs upright," announced the purser, "and fasten your seatbelts." We were being put on notice that we were coming down for a landing at Toronto's Pearson International Airport. When you have been away for several weeks, it is always a great feeling to come home. After Argentina, we'd visited Peru and Ecuador. The experiences left me with overwhelmingly good feelings, but one sad thought stood out; where was Harry?

That little penguin had stolen my heart. He couldn't fly in the air but he could certainly fly in the water. In my mind I could see him flying around like a jet plane in those chilly blue waters off the coast of Patagonia. I know that he would have loved to be able to fly home with Lillian and me on this big jet. In my mind this time, it was me calling to Harry in my bass tone, "Fly with me."

WALTER W. GOWING

CHAPTER 2

FAIRY PENGUINS

It is a long flight to Australia from Canada, no matter whether you live in Halifax or Vancouver. The investment in time is rewarding when you consider the Aussies are enjoying beautiful summer weather during our cold winter. Fly with me, and let's enjoy the warm sun, sandy beaches, and some uniquely down-under experiences.

My wife Lillian and I were in Australia for a few weeks before visiting the country's most southern city of Melbourne. From there, we took a bus further south, crossing a causeway to reach a most unusual place called Phillips Island in the state of New South Wales. The sometimes wild and ferocious Bass Strait separates Phillips Island, which is attached by causeway to the Australian continent, from the island state of Tasmania. Lillian and I have reluctantly sailed the strait a couple of times. We were fortunate enough to traverse the waters on a moderate to calm sea, though the strait is known to turn many passengers' stomachs upside down when the waters are rough.

I have heard it said that Tasmania has more golf courses than people, but that's the way the Aussies talk –

eh, mate. Tasmania is the only home of the Tasmanian devil, a bear-like nocturnal, flesh-eating creature that you would not want to tangle with if you're planning to survive.

We finally arrived at Phillips Island and had a delicious lobster dinner at Taylor's Restaurant. The lobster was marvelous and fresh from the nearby cold Southern Ocean.

The reason we wanted to visit Phillips Island was to see the cutest penguins in the world, commonly known as Fairy penguins. These little gaffers never grow any taller than the distance from your kneecap to the ground. Most of the Fairy penguins never reach more than 14-18 inches in height. The scientific name of these birds is Eudyptula minor, meaning small good diver. They are often referred to as the "Little Penguin." Their sleek, oily plumage is a blue-grey colour with a white under part. You can hear them talk to one another with their grunts, yaps, and brays. The females lay two eggs, but both parents share the brooding for 36 days. When hatched, newborns take up to 56 days before they are ready to enter the cold, rough waters that ply the southern shore of the Australian continent.

After our dinner we headed to Summerland's Beach, where at dusk, the smallest penguins in the world waddle up the beach to their burrows on the hillside. After a long day in the water filling up with food – really filling up, as they become care boxes for their young ones at home – the adult penguins come ashore. Individual penguins remain in the rolling surf along the shoreline until 20 or 30 of them are gathered together and then, as a group they attempt to make it across a fairly wide beach to the hillside. Once on the grassy slopes, they are safe from the predators in the air above the sandy beach.

While we watched this action repeat itself over and over again, we noticed their enemy in the sky, circling around and around watching the little penguins gather in the water before making a break for the hillside. They have a much better chance of making it home if they stick together when they are in the open. A single penguin becomes a target for a hungry hawk circling above. There are 27 different types of birds of prey in Australia, all with hooked beaks and sharp, curved talons. The hawks are powerful enough to swoop down and pick up a Little Penguin.

Lillian and I were sitting partway up the hillside looking down as though we were at the Coliseum in Rome. I could imagine Caesar calling for the release of the lions on the poor defenseless Christians in the open ring below. The hawks were every bit as dangerous to those little penguins as the lions were to the frightened people they were about to attack.

On one occasion, the birds emerged from the water in a straggly formation with considerable space between them. Suddenly, the sharp-eyed hawk darted downward toward the vulnerable creatures. The hawk was like a British Spitfire in wartime, diving on an enemy plane. In the blink of an eye, those tiny penguins turned and were back in the ocean in a flash. The hawk swooped down over the deserted beach without catching its dinner. We were eagerly cheering for the penguins, but then what does the hawk do for a meal?

We waited a few minutes and when the water became crowded with penguins, we watched them make another attempt to escape the rolling waves and cross the battle zone to safety. This time, they left the water shoulder to shoulder as they marched across the beach without being attacked by the hungry hawk in the sky. They quickly made it to their burrows to regurgitate food for their young. As we walked along the pathway back up the hill, we had to be careful not step on these wonderful little friends. Not to mention, you can't touch them because our human hands could remove their oily coat, tampering with their waterproofing. Seeing the Fairy Penguins is truly seeing Nature at her best.

The next day in Melbourne, we were back on the rails again. Lillian and I had a most delightful dinner, Victorian style, on the streets of the city. The dining facilities at the Colonial Tramcar Restaurant was truly the most unique we'd seen at any place in the world. Two tramcars connected, fully equipped with a kitchen, plush red velvet seating areas with tables for two or four, and a chef who could create the most exquisite foods that even folks at Buckingham Palace would love to eat.

As we travelled on the tramcar around the streets of

Australia's second largest city, on the same tracks as the streetcars, we enjoyed champagne, rare wine, and a six-course meal fit for a queen. And to only enhance the theme of our journey, the tuxedo-dressed waiters serving our dinner on fine china reminded me of my friends at the rookery. An evening to remember, even London's Savoy Hotel couldn't top it.

WALTER W. GOWING

CHAPTER 3

ON THE ROCKS

"Look out!" I shouted as I tumbled from one giant rock to another down a slope that was going to end in a mixture of wild churning waters from two different oceans at the tip of South Africa. Why I yelled was anybody's guess, because there wasn't anyone around with the exception of a couple dozen penguins.

This could be a matter of life or death. Even that daredevil Evel Knievel, the world-renowned motorcycle jumper from Butte, Montana would surely hesitate to jump these enormous rocks at the edge of two angry oceans. The American stuntman still holds the record for the most number of bones fractured in his career. It's 433, in case you were looking to break it.

Just like our many trips in this exciting world of wonders, this one would create moments of its own. It all started when Lillian and I took a long flight from Toronto via London's Heathrow Airport in England to Cape Town, South Africa. It is one long flight. After landing, it didn't take me long to get into some mess of trouble.

On the south shore of the continent, I found myself face-to-face with a flock of flightless birds. These South

African birds stood motionless on a pile of gigantic rocks as I stumbled and went flying through the air right by them. There wasn't even time to wave. Their expressionless faces appeared not to care that I was in flight and they were shackled to the ground.

Though expressionless, their eyes stared with curiously. Even at a disastrous time like this, I could hear their squawky voices. They were probably communicating with one another, chuckling about a crazy human trying to fly. After all, they were birds who couldn't fly. Why would a wingless human be able to accomplish such a feat?

At a time like this, my main concern was protecting my trusty little camera that has been with me around the world. Words and stories I can replace, but the photographic evidence of my exploits are like diamonds in the rough. The card in my camera had shots of a unique fishing village, Hout Bay, and some of its locals.

Lillian was in some of the pictures. I had shots taken from Table Mountain in Cape Town, looking across the waters to Robben Island where Nelson Mandela was imprisoned for most of his 28 years behind bars. Another great picture on the precious card was the restricted entrance to the farm prison Drakenstein, the correctional institution where Mandela walked out a free man on February 11, 1990.

I mean, I was risking my life! The Evel Knievel of saving my memories.
There I was, scrambling to get back onto my feet on those slippery smooth rocks the size of refrigerators. I

was trying to avoid sliding farther down the jagged slope into the swirling waters below. It was a dangerous place where the Indian and Atlantic oceans crash together in an angry, foaming collage. Not far from the Cape of Good Hope and just east of False Bay where I went to look at a colony of penguins.

I can't go on without explaining a little of False Bay's history. This unusual bay has an extraordinary wind condition. The early trading ships plying the dangerous windy southern route around the Cape of Good Hope, an area where many ships were lost as they were blown onto the submerged rocks, would discover this inviting bay with the winds blowing into it. A ship's Captain would sail into the bay for restocking food and water, but would end up trapped for several months at a time. The strange winds blowing into the bay wouldn't change direction for six months, when they'd change course and blow out of the bay. Sailing vessels needed a favourable wind to get back out of the bay, or they'd be stuck. Several ships at a time could be found in the bay, waiting for the wind to work with them. You can see how this inlet was appropriately named False Bay.

Just to keep the record straight, the real southern tip of Africa is about 150 km east of the Cape of Good Hope, at Cape Agulhas. Between these two capes is where the Atlantic and Indian Oceans meet.

I motored down from Cape Town, my favourite city in the world, to the most southwestern point of the continent. Cape Town, with a population of three million, is where the South African parliament meets, though the administrative capital of the country is Pretoria.

I have two favourite spots in Cape Town that I visit each trip. The first is the waterfront where most of the land is actually reclaimed land from the sea. It is a delightful place to sit under an umbrella with Lillian and enjoy a delicious lunch at dockside. You are surrounded on one side by great gleaming cruise ships, freighters and tankers, and on the other side by petite sailboats and motor launches. As the harbour waters lap against the dock just inches away from where you sit, you can see the majestic Table Mountain in the background, overlooking the city and harbour. What a fabulous place to be as live music fills the air.

Small groups of musicians stroll the area playing everything from Dixieland to classical. Plucking the strings of guitars or playing trumpets add to the charm of Cape Town's harbour. My favourite groups always include a banjo player. The twang of the strings on a banjo are invigorating, inviting you to snap your fingers and tap your toes.

The second favourite Cape Town spot is Table Mountain. It is a sleeping giant resting behind the hustle and bustle of people working and living between the sheer rock mountainside and the rolling waters of an ocean below. There is a long cable car ride up the side of the mountain. It is like climbing to the top of the world. The view on a clear day from the top of Table Mountain is spectacular. You can see for miles. Automobiles in the city below look like miniature toy cars running around. Off in the distance is Robben Island, along with

Mandela, the piece of land rising from the ocean depths was home to hundreds of prisoners whose only crime was asking the government for equality.

The Cape of Good Hope is often very windy and the angry waters rushing in from the Atlantic over the hidden rocks offshore have taken many sailing ships to their watery graves. In the old days, when sailing vessels carried precious cargo of spice from the East and had to make the long water route from India and China to England and Europe, they had to sail around the Cape. Today's modern ships can cut the distance in two by going through the Suez Canal in Egypt.

Now was not the time to be thinking about man's creative wonders of the world. I was still flying through the air over those giant rocks at the penguin colony. There I was, still grappling for some kind of security as I tumbled through the air, really hoping for a safe landing. I reached out with my left arm and with the tips of my fingers, grabbed the sharp edge of a huge rock below me. I came to a sudden stop in mid-air. Down I crashed onto my stomach onto the flat surface of a rock that knocked the breath right out of me. Gasping for air I turned, and low and behold, those penguins were still staring at me like it was the best free show on the South African coast.

After a few moments of calmness, as I began to breathe normally again, I pulled myself up on my hands and knees. I was only one great rock away from the churning waters below. It was lapping like a pack of hungry hyenas, waiting for my next misstep.

I came to see penguins. I came to take pictures of penguins. I came to write about penguins. What I didn't come for, was to perform a most embarrassing stunt right before all of those penguins.

When I got back to the hotel, I allowed myself to have a drink – straight up, not on the rocks.

CHAPTER 4

BIG BIRD

It's a bird, it's a plane, it's Superman – so goes the introduction to one of the most successful Hollywood features to ever come out of a comic book series, and found in nearly every North American home

In 1999, I interviewed Eddie Bockser, the guardian of Superman at Warner Bros. Studio in Burbank, California. Eddie had worked for Warner Bros. for 35 years and retired in 1994. I found him back at the studio as a volunteer at their museum. He spent most of his working life at Warner Bros., first starting in the mailroom and then moving on to just about every department on the movie lot.

"When I started here," Eddie explained, "I didn't have any relatives working here." I guess he felt an explanation was necessary about how he landed a gig at one of the world's major motion picture studios. In the early days, you really needed to have a brother, an uncle or a cousin on the inside of most studios to get a job.

Eddie was born in the Bronx, a borough in the northeast section of New York City. When he was seven years old, he saw the movie *The Charge of the Light Brigade* and he was hooked. Michael Curtiz directed that film in

1936 and became one of Hollywood's most prominent directors. Curtiz directed some of the industry's biggest hits at the time, including two of the best musicals *Yankee Doodle Dandy (*1942) and *White Christmas* (1954) filmed at Paramount Studios. Curtiz won an Oscar in 1943 for Best Director for *Casablanca*.

Casablanca starring Humphrey Bogart, Ingrid Bergman and Paul Henreid, was shot completely at the Warner Bros. facility in Burbank. There was one scene, however, where the film crew used nearby Van Nuys Airport so that they could film real full-size airplanes. Other notable actors in the project included Claude Rains, Sydney Greenstreet and Peter Lorre. *Casablanca* won three Academy Awards.

Many of the movie's scenes took place in Rick's Café. The only real Rick's Café was on the Hollywood set at Warner Bros. An American businesswoman opened a café in Casablanca to capitalize on the popularity of the movie. Lillian and I have been to Casablanca on two occasions and checked out the imitation Rick's. It is interesting, but not the real thing.

Memories were important to Eddie as he recalled some interesting times over the years at the studio. He told me about the time he snuck through the back door to attend a dinner in honour of Robert Preston after wrapping the film *Music Man*. He wasn't invited, but that didn't stop him from being a part of the celebrations.

Canadian Lorne Green was one of Eddie's heroes. He met Green after the television series *Bonanza* moved from Paramount to Warner Bros. He said Green treated the production crew with respect. He was like a father to the younger actors on the set.

Eddie knew what was going on behind the scenes on open sets, too. He said two of the biggest scrappers on the lot were Bette Davis and studio big shot Jack Warner. Eddie said, "They fought like cat and dog."

In 1935, Davis won her first Oscar for best actress in the film *Dangerous*. Warner capitalized on this success by rushing Davis into several mediocre films. Finally Davis refused to do a film called *God's Country and the Woman*. Warner suspended her and fined her $5,000 per week. Davis went to England to make a movie for another studio and Warner Bros. took her to court, claiming she was in violation of her contract.

The studio won, but garnered so much negative publicity that they ended up giving Davis the money to pay her court costs. In addition, the studio gave her a role alongside Humphrey Bogart in *Marked Woman*.

Warner Bros. Museum opened two years before my conversation with 70-year old Eddie Bockser, now the head keeper of the museum's treasures. Actually, Lillian and I attended the grand opening of this remarkable collection of movie memorabilia and the history of Warner Bros. Having a second look was even better as more items were added to continually document the decades of Warner moviemaking magic.

Items on display included the piano and chandelier from Rick's Café in *Casablanca*, Natalie Wood's gown from *Gypsy*, and Mel Gibson and Danny Glover's *Lethal Weapon* outfits.

One of my favorite displays was on *Superman*. Eddie proudly showed me the production drawings from the 1978 film. Unfortunately, what the display doesn't tell you, is that the creator of the hero was a Canadian. Joe Shuster was born in Toronto in 1914. He moved with his family to the United States in 1923 and teamed up with writer Jerry Siegel in 1938 to produce the film Superman story for Action Comics. The drawings were Shuster's, while Siegel wrote the storyline.

I was sorry to hear that Shuster ended up in a nursing home in southern California without the wealth that should have been his. As old age crept up on Shuster and he couldn't draw one of America's favourite heroes anymore, it was sort of like being cast aside. Shuster was not a wealthy man, in part because he didn't own the character rights to Superman.

The Broadway musical *It's a Bird, It's a Plane, It's Superman* reminded me of a wild adventure that I had with a couple of pals in South Africa.

The bird part was certainly true. It was a big one, an ostrich. It all happened when we got ourselves involved with an ostrich farm near the town of Oudtshoorn.

The plane was a crowded South African Airways flight we made from London to Cape Town.

Superman? Well, that certainly covers the bravery part of our act, or the careless stupidity of Canucks in the face of danger.

Our small group of adventurers included our leader, Rob Bullas, my wife Lillian, a couple of retired school teachers and an assortment of other fun-loving characters. From my hometown of Cambridge, we had the delightful Murray Jull, a retired Galt Collegiate Institute mathematics teacher and an outstanding organist and pianist in the community. I've been told that math and music go together. If your numbers don't jive in math, it's much like misreading music and hitting all the wrong notes. Jull is the organist at Avenue Road Baptist Church and the pianist for the world-renowned Cambridge Kiwanis Boys Choir, directed by James Kropf.

Our other teacher from Cambridge was in the elementary system and spent many years at Preston Parkway Public School. Besides the school curriculum, Larry Rawlings devoted a great deal of time to extra activities at the school.

According to Lillian's journal, we travelled through the Du Toits Kloof Pass of a mountain range, and at one point passed through a tunnel that was two and a half miles long. When exiting the tunnel, we found vineyards and farms rich in colour. We passed through the little villages of Worcester and Robertson, stopping at Ladismith, a small hamlet where Lillian purchased three antique silver spoons. We enjoyed meeting the local people. Late that afternoon, we arrived in Oudtshoorn, a pleasant and clean town with mostly white buildings with red roofs.

In Oudsthoorn we stayed at the Queen's Hotel on Baron van Reede Street, where King George VI and his family stayed in 1947. It was a small hotel but if it was good enough for King George, it was good enough for us. It was a very fine place with white pillars across the front. At the back of the hotel was a beautiful garden with fruit trees in the courtyard. Next door to the hotel, I bought Lillian an ostrich egg. The hand-painted egg has the pictures of the "Big 5" animals of Africa; the elephant, buffalo, lion, leopard and rhino. How do you carry a giant-sized egg back to Canada? Well-packed and very carefully!

The next day we were off to the ostrich farm. This is where our travelling partners, the crazy Canucks, thought they were still playing ice hockey and living dangerously just to show that Canadians can do it. Before the big event of the day, we were shown around the farm and learned a great deal about ostriches. A person can stand on an ostrich egg and it will not break if it is on sand and not on a hard surface. The reason is that the sand is soft and allows the egg to sink into it like a cushion. Usually three to six females lay their eggs in the same nest that has been dug by a male. Each hen may lay as many as 10 eggs. The male sits on the nest and protects the eggs at night. During the day, the dominant hen keeps the eggs warm. Ostriches can live up to 40 years.

The ostrich is the world's largest bird and can stand as high as eight feet tall. It has two toes, both with sharp nails on each. Both its toes and a hard beak can become dangerous weapons when it is cornered or protecting its eggs. The giant bird can sprint as fast as 70 kilometres per hour. This big bird cannot fly.

It was a very educational and pleasant time visiting the farm where hundreds of ostriches at various stages in life were available to see. They are raised for their meat, and their skins make leather goods like purses, belts, shoes and jackets. Their plumes are still sold but are not as in high demand as they were several decades ago.

The time had come when our farm guide stopped at what looked like wooden steps leading up to a small platform against the fence line. He gathered everyone together and asked if there were any volunteers to ride an ostrich. I immediately put up my hand without thinking. Everyone applauded, but I still wasn't sure if I heard the question correctly. Did the guide really say he wanted someone to ride an ostrich? What did I volunteer for this time?

The guide said we needed more than one person for this contest. Susan Robertson of North Bay, Ontario was in our group and raised her arm to indicate that she would volunteer. Susan was a brave woman.

The guide said he would need one more person to complete the race. That's when Larry Rawlings volunteered Murray Jull, claiming Murray would do the riding while he, Larry that is, took the pictures.

The competition was to see if one rider at a time could make it around a very large field riding on the back of an ostrich. The guide said the jockeys would go in the order they volunteered. That put me first without an opportunity to really see what this adventure was all about.

I climbed the steps, just like a condemned prisoner climbing the gallows to reach the level of the hangman. The handlers had already secured a very large bird and placed a sock-like item over its head. The ostrich was very quiet and still. Did I mention how big this ostrich was? Maybe I'll say it a few more times. The handlers took a hold of me and helped me straddle the bird that weighed about 345 pounds (156 kg). I thought that all this big bird had to do was stop out there in the field, toss me off and then sit on me. If this happened, I would look like a pancake, flattened even more by a steamroller.

Next, they had me tuck my feet under each wing of the big bird and put both my hands solidly around its long neck.

"You are ready for takeoff," shouted one of the handlers, almost implying that we were going to fly. I had never heard of a flying ostrich, but in these days of jet propulsion, you could probably expect anything. They pulled off the bag from the ostrich's head and instantly, like torching a match to a rocket, off went the ostrich with me hanging on for dear life. It followed the fence line as I hung on tightly with my hands around its neck and my feet somehow still tucked under its big wings. At one point I thought that if the bird were to find an opening in the fence, we wouldn't stop for 100 miles (160 km).

Turning at the corners of this Texas-sized wilderness field, it was a little tricky, as you had to sway with the bird when it made the corner without slowing down. I could hear the crowd roaring as we headed for the third corner of the field. It felt like coming down the stretch at the Kentucky Derby. If the Derby crowd could see me now, they wouldn't be cheering and shouting, they would be laughing.

Lillian and I have been to the magnificent racing facility at Churchill Downs in Louisville, Kentucky. They tell me that Derby tickets are the most coveted in all of thoroughbred racing. People from around the world attend this racing event that has been taking place annually since 1875. I don't think the racing officials at Churchill Downs would allow an ostrich to run the track at their prestigious facility.

The handlers were able to corner the bird following my speedy ride, and were able to get a bag back over its head and lead it to the stand that I started at. I climbed off its back and wobbled down the steps to congratulatory greetings from the crowd. If they ever open a track for ostrich racing, I'm experienced, but count me out. I would just like to be known as a retired ostrich jockey.

Now it was Susan's turn to follow the same routine that I had just completed. She mounted the big bird with the sock over its head. When the handlers took the head cover off the bird, it took off like it was shot from a canon. Around the field she travelled, and garnered applause when she finished her ride. There was just one problem in getting Susan off the ostrich once it was up against the steps. Susan was still hanging on with both hands to the ostrich's neck. The handlers almost had to pry her hands from the bird and untangle her legs from under the wings. She was prepared to stay aboard her ride at any speed.

Finally it was Murray's turn to ride the over-energetic giant bird around the field. Up the steps he climbed. Murray surely would have felt more at home if it had been Carnegie Hall or the Hollywood Bowl with a piano waiting atop those steps.

Murray set danger aside as he swung his leg over the ostrich and tucked his knees under the wings. He placed his musically inclined fingers, the ones meant for flying over the ivory keys of a piano, around the big bird's neck. Just as the handlers were removing the sock from the head of the bird and it was ready to race like a Derby horse, Murray removed his right hand from the bird's neck and waved to the crowd. Where was the band? An appropriate loud and stirring musical accompaniment would have added to the excitement of the moment.

At Churchill Downs they always play "My Old Kentucky Home" to open the day's racing schedule. Murray would probably know the song has a line in it about the birds making music. There was no music that day on the ostrich farm in South Africa. There were no television cameras, only Larry with his little camera taking pictures of this monumental event.

The ostrich was gone and so was Murray. Across the field the ostrich darted with Murray on its back, just like the two of them were chasing a fox in an English hunting scene.

One of the onlookers shouted, "Mine that bird!" I'll bet Murray didn't know that at the running of the Kentucky Derby in 2009, the thoroughbred racehorse that won was named "Mine That Bird."

It was Murray and the ostrich right down the finish line. "Mine That Bird" retired from racing after accumulating earning of $2,228,637 during his three-year racing career. Murray retired from ostrich racing after one race without any cash prize, just memories of his first and final ride around the track near Oudtshoorn, South Africa. And Larry, well he probably got another 100 pictures of ostriches to add to the million or more pictures that he'd already taken on this trip.

Who says ostriches can't fly? At the speed those giants made it around that South African field, they sure fooled us.

Surrounded by thousands of Magellanic penguins in Punta Tombo, Walter was warmly approached by one little tyke who wanted to become a friend. This is one of the world's largest rookeries.

"I'm sorry Harry but I can't take you with me," Walter said to his new-found friend in Argentina's dry, desolate region of Patagonia. The penguins enjoy six months of the year before taking to the Atlantic Ocean for a swim north. Walter wouldn't be joining Harry for the chilly swim.

Some of the incredible tango dancers at the ranch near Buenos Aires.

The tango is a syncopated ballroom dance that originated in Argentina. The performers use long dramatic gliding movements and abrupt pauses with changes in direction in 2/4 and 4/4 timing.

Walter (above) and Murray Jull (below) are off to the races, riding ostriches and looking for a championship title. These birds can't fly, but they can run at speeds of up to 70 km/hour.

PART TWO

PLANES AND TRAINS

CHAPTER FIVE

COLD, COLD, COLD

We had a choice: fly into Antarctica with all its ice and snow or ride the rails in Argentina heading north from the little town of Ushuaia, located on the landmass of Tierra del Fuego. This land is separated from the main continent by the Straight of Magellan near the tip of South America. I wanted no part of the cold wind and the frozen landscape that Antarctica offered. We decided to take a cozy little train with its red and black steam engine and pretty blue coaches. We were going to travel north to warmer weather. Lillian had enough of the cold climate around Cape Horn and passing through Beagle Channel near Prince William Island. This was not bikini country, break out the parka coats. Both of us agreed that the train was the way to travel out of Ushuaia.

The Ferrocarril Austral Fueguino (in English, the Southern Fueguean Railway) took us on an interesting ride through the Tierra del Fuego National Park. This rail line has a fantastic history as it sprung from an early whaling station in Ushuaia. English missionaries established the colony in the 1870s. In 1894, the Argentine Navy took control of the settlement and turned it into a penal colony. Prisoners were brought here from as far away as Europe. The penal colony was known as the "Prison for Relapsed Felons" and at one time had over 1,000 prisoners. The prisoners built the narrow gage railway that Lillian and I chose to ride in Argentina.

The scenery was beautiful with its deep green forests and in the background, high snow-covered mountains. Many small streams flowed out of the mountains and through culverts under the tracks. It was a fascinating train ride with all its historical glamour. The clickety-clack of the train's steel wheels as they circled over and over again on the steel rails had some kind of musical tone that could put you to sleep. The rails were mounted on a less than smooth track bed.

When the train stopped at each station, I jumped from the passenger car and ran up and down the platform almost missing the train once when it pulled out without tooting its whistle. On occasion the train had to stop to switch tracks or remove a tree branch from across the railway line. In some areas those pesky beavers, you know, the adorable little creatures that come from Canada, had used their sharp teeth to take down a good sized tree. This occurred more than once as we rambled along in the shadow of some pretty high mountains. All of the peaks were capped in snow. Cold snow! Why was I running about at every opportunity? Cold, really cold!

A number of the windows in the train had the panes of glass missing. There was no door at one end of the coach we were riding in. The air from the moving train just whistled through the coach like you were standing at Canada's coldest intersection, the corner of Portage and Main in Winnipeg, Manitoba. When the cold northwest wind is coming at you like a herd of buffalo on the run, you should know enough to find a better spot in Western Canada. Did I already say it was cold? In southern Argentina, the cold chill on that train made the coldest day in Winnipeg feel like a hot, tropical day in Jamaica.

Poor Lillian. There she was, sitting in that pretty blue train coach with the wind blowing her hair. It was like sitting in front of a giant fan and being surrounded by blocks of ice. She wasn't dressed for this kind of expedition. She wasn't the only one, either. I never expected it to be so cold on a train. This was a train without a heating system. Only the engineer and the fireman stoking the boiler were able to keep warm on the train. Remember: this was supposed to be the comfortable warm train ride in place of the flight into the ice-covered continent around the South Pole. If we had taken that plane south, the plan was to drop us off at a weather station for a couple of days. The problem was that if the weather deteriorated, the plane might not be able to pick us up for one, two or three weeks. Maybe even longer.

Riding this South American train under these cold conditions was a new experience. Look at it this way, it was a new adventure, but why didn't someone tell us about the conditions so we could have better prepared ourselves for the frigid ride? We just had to persevere the cold until the end of the rail ride.

We were headed to warmer temperatures, but in the meantime, we felt that we might freeze to death before we reached any semblance of warmer air. Between stops I would sit with my arm around Lillian in an attempt to keep her from becoming as stiff as an icicle. At one point, I believed that they would have to use a blowtorch or a flame-thrower to thaw us out before we'd be able to disembark.

There was another alternative back in Ushuaia. Riding this train, we began to wonder if going to Antarctica on a warm ship may have been a better idea. Maybe we should have given it a little more consideration.

Lillian took my picture with a young female officer back in Ushuaia who was serving on a beautiful red and white ship, midsize in build (the ship, I mean). The officer was charming, friendly and pleasant to talk with as we chatted in that brisk cold.

"If the whole crew were as gracious as this young woman, it would be a pleasure to sail aboard this ship," I told Lillian.

It was a Canadian ship called the M/S Explorer and it was owned by G.A.P. Adventures (Great Adventure People), a travel company headquartered in Toronto. G.A.P. changed its name in 2011 to G Adventures. The company was founded and is still headed by Bruce Poon Tip, an entrepreneur, adventurer and genius in bringing people together around the world. If the country you want to travel to is on the map, there's a good chance G Adventures operates there. It runs adventures on all seven continents. G Adventures is a Cinderella story of one man's dream of taking adventures off-the-beaten track to where the real people in a country work and live.

I talked with the young woman for some time because she was serving on a Canadian ship so far from home. She invited me aboard to look over the ship as it was in the harbour to take on supplies.

Monday, February 28, 2005 was the day I stood on the deck of the MS Explorer in the Port of Ushuaia. This small city at the southernmost tip of Argentina has a population of 56,000, and is about 650 km (450 miles) southwest of the Falkland Islands. Ushuaia is considered the southernmost city in the world. Its highest elevation within the town limits is only 23 metres (75 feet) above sea level. If you like heights, all you need to do is look beyond the town. There, in the background, the mountains rise high up into the blue skies with snow-covered peaks. Across the Beagle Channel is the small community of Puerto Williams with a population of less than 3,000. The Chilean town also claims to hold the geographical title of the world's southernmost community.

The first recorded settlement in the Strait of Magellan was established in 1587 by John Williams Wilson, a Britisher. The current settlement was organized in 1953 and is made up of a large number of Chilean naval personnel. The Chilean Navy operates the harbour, the hospital, and the Guardiamarina Zanartu Airport.

Although you could see your breath at times because of the nippy cold air, the sun was shining brightly overhead. The Canadian MS Explorer, the first cruise ship built to ply the cold icy waters off Antarctica, was undoubtedly a beautiful vessel. The ship was built by Uudenkaupungin Telakka in Finland and launched in 1969. It was originally commissioned and operated by Lars-Eric Lindblad, the famous Swedish explorer. During its lifetime, the ship changed ownership many times before ending up the property of G.A.P. Shipping in 2004. Its record included running aground near La Plaza Point, Antarctica on February 11, 1972 with Lindblad aboard. On Christmas Day 1979, the ship ran aground again off Vicky Island in the Antarctic and the Chilean Navy icebreaker, the Piloto Pardo, rescued 140 passengers from the ship. Under German ownership in 1989, the 73-metre long (239 feet) Explorer turned rescuer when it came to the aid of an Argentinian supply ship in Antarctica. It rescued the crew from the stranded ship that was wedged on a rock ledge of Anvers Island. The Explorer was often referred to by its nickname "The Little Red Ship" by its passengers and crew.

When all was said and done, we made the choice to take that chilly train ride running north from Ushuaia. I can't resist trains or the prospect of warmer weather. The ship was heading south toward the South Pole and lots of cold, cold ice.

Turn the clock ahead about three years and you find us back home in Cambridge, Ontario. It was a great shock to hear of the tragic sinking of the MS Explorer. The adventurous ship had gone to its waterlogged grave in the frigid depths of the waters surrounding the South Pole. The vessel struck an iceberg on November 23, 2007 and sunk to the bottom of the Antarctic Ocean.

The only remaining evidence of the ship was an oil

slick about 80 km east of King George Island. It was estimated that about 190,000 litres of diesel, 24,000 litres of lubricant, and 980 litres of gasoline were onboard the vessel when the ship's hull was punctured by the fateful iceberg and it began taking on water. My God, I thought, it was the Titanic all over again.

The MS Explorer was carrying 154 passengers and crew when misfortune struck, making it necessary to abandon ship some time after midnight. In the dark of the night, the temperature was around -5 Celcius as the lifeboats and Zodiacs bobbed up and down in the ice-laden water. At 6:30 a.m., the first of two rescue ships arrived. The National Geographic Endeavour and the Norwegian Norde Norge took the passengers, including 10 Canadians, and the crew who by all reports, carried out their duties extremely well.

The brave Explorer tried to stay afloat, but as water poured into the ship, it turned on its side before its death plunge to the bottom of the ocean, some 1,460 metres below the surface. Although the ship had several watertight compartments, striking the hard ice that punctured the ship below the waterline required emergency pumps to discharge the water back into the ocean. The pumps were unable to operate because the ship's power had gone off and the pumps required electricity to function. It was surely a frightening moment for the passengers when the captain gave the order to "abandon ship" and take to the lifeboats and dinghies.

The MS Explorer, a brave and proud little ship, is one to never be forgotten, especially by those passengers and members of the crew. Time heals and a new ship plies the waters of Antarctica. In 2008, Toronto's G Adventures acquired another ship to take the place of the Explorer.

The newly acquired ship, built in 1972 in Denmark, switched owners several times and sailed under the names of Kattgat, Tiger and Alandsfarjan before becoming the MS Expedition with G. Adventures.

Looking back to that day when Lillian and I were in Ushuaia, a small city with many people living in prefab houses that were made in Canada, we recalled the crazy little wood-burning stove in the tiny station. Popular sports in the community were soccer and ice hockey – Canada, eh! We think we made the right choice of train over Antarctic cruise.

In retrospect, I think our adventurous ride on the Southern Fueguean Railway was the best option of the three possibilities. The train showed us an area of the world where few people get the opportunity to ride a train, the most southern in the world. I'm glad we did it.

CHAPTER 6

PUFFING BILLY

Fly with me to Australia. You see, I love riding trains, but you can't take a train from North America to Australia. We did have a choice between sailing on a ship to go Down Under or choosing to fly on a jet airplane. We took the jet. It was much faster.

Arriving in the land of kangaroos and koalas, we were now ready to hit the rails.

Let me tell you about one old huffing and puffing happy little steam engine that pulled our passenger cars on a rickety rail line south of Melbourne, Australia. We will never forget "Puffing Billy," the old narrow gauge steam train that chugs along in the state of New South Wales in the southeast of Australia. It has been running since 1900. This century-old train runs from Gembrook to Belgrave, just outside of Melbourne, the state's capital city. Billy was much like the Southern Fueguean Railway in Argentina except the weather in Australia was a great deal warmer than the cold Antarctic air that swept over the southern Argentine landscape. The worst Billy could do is let its wood-burning boiler pump out heavy dark smoke once in awhile that could drift in through the open windows and clog up a person's breathing for a minute or two.

The sound of a steam engine whistle is an attraction that makes one stop everything and listen. Down Under, farmers stop their tractors to listen to the charming call of the steam train. It was this way when the Canadian National Railroad and the Canadian Pacific Railway competed for passengers and freight to haul across the vast Dominion of Canada. The sound of a whistle from a diesel locomotive is harsh, cold and mechanical. Puffing Billy made no mistake when it blew off steam sounding its whistle. It was the true sound of a steam engine.

Puffing Billy is a black engine with a large headlight mounted at the front on top of its big round boiler. There is usually steam shooting out from under its carriage while white fluffy clouds of smoke swirl from its tall stack. It puffs along through the countryside, pulling about six reddish-coloured passenger cars. It is a thrill to see Puffing Billy chug along the track and an even greater thrill to be on one if its cars.

There is always passenger excitement when Puffing Billy toots its whistle when crossing the heritage trestle bridge near Selby. This historic wooden structure reminds one of a notorious plot to blow up the bridge in the film *The Bridge on the River Kwai*. This Columbia Pictures Oscar-winning movie was produced in 1956 by Sam Spiegel and starred the well-known Hollywood actor William Holden. Some of the older passengers riding Puffing Billy's railcars told me that they had seen the movie several times and when crossing the Selby Bridge, they felt a tingle and tightened up recalling the explosion that blew up the bridge in the movie.

Puffing Billy has some special night runs that offer an evening of great jazz music by the Mast Gully Quartet and a dinner served at a train stop at the end of the line. Returning home on the same track, the passengers are served tea, coffee and Australian wine with that extra touch of fine Australian dinner chocolates. And if jazz is not your choice, there are the nights you can ride Puffing Billy to the end of the line for dinner and a murder mystery with the Gemco Players Community Theatre. It is a fun-packed stop where you will want to find out "who dunnit" in the rustic old Nobelious Packing Shed while enjoying a delightful dinner. Then, hop back on the train for your return trip to Belgrave Station. At Christmas time, Santa Claus rides the train and gives presents to the children onboard. Oh yes, remember that you're in Australia and the adults get sherry and wine.

It was March, the fall season Down Under, that we took Puffing Billy through the lush foliage along with the sights and sounds of hundreds of colourful birds. The variety of plants and birds really make this trip very enjoyable. The incredibly friendly Rosellas added to the attraction of taking this train. Before getting on the train, they would land on your head or shoulders, begging for a cookie or a piece of bread. There were hundreds of Rosellas, a member of the parrot family, that swarmed around like fighter planes attacking in a war movie. The birds were harmless and friendly. They were the size of seagulls and this made some people very nervous when they attempted to land on their shoulders. It seemed amazing that they were not afraid of humans. I must say that some people were afraid of them. The colourful plumage of the Rosellas is a sharp rich brightness that extends from its deep red head to its belly and underparts. Its back is mottled red and black and it has cheek patches, tail and wing tips of a deep royal blue. It is a noisy bird. Its chattering could drive a person to wear earplugs. Unlike many humans today, the Rosellas mate for life. The female incubates four of five white eggs and when the chicks hatch, both parents feed them and provide parental care.

After Puffing Billy, we boarded a bus that took us further southwest on the Australian continent, away from Melbourne. On our way to the coast, we stopped to watch and mingle with some kangaroos. They come in all sizes, but the big ones stretch over six feet tall and can be a little dangerous at times. If you have any food in your pockets you had better surrender it to the larger ones before they knock you to the ground and take it from you. These were mostly the Eastern Grey kangaroos. They live on the grasslands, in the scrubland and in wooded areas. You find this variety of the kangaroo from the inland plains to the east coast. Their habitat extends pretty well from northern Tasmania and the southern tip of Australia to as far north as the city of Cairns and the offshore Great Barrier Reef.

Lillian loved the little kangaroos but unfortunately they all grow to be big ones. We saw red kangaroos in other areas across Australia and they grow as high as six feet tall. Her favourite animal is really the wallaby, a member of the Macropodidae family, smaller than kangaroos but very similar looking to a small one. We saw many of these in north Australia, especially around Darwin.

If a number of kangaroos are assembled, they are not to be called a herd or a flock, but a mob. They gather in a mob to feed in the late evenings and early morning hours as they find the daytime is usually too warm for them. There is nothing more loveable than to see a female kangaroo with a Joey, a young kangaroo, sticking its head out of its mother's pouch. A newborn joey will spend up to eight months of its young life in its mother's pouch.

Eventually we made it back to Melbourne where we could not leave the city without visiting some of its historic flea markets and bazaars. Melbourne probably has more of these institutions than any other city in the world. If you are searching for something old, new, unusual or exotic, then you are almost guaranteed to find it in one of the tourist-drawing retail places in the city.

Some of these markets are located in historic buildings like the giant Queen Victoria Market, which first opened on March 20, 1878. There is more to do than just indoor shopping as outside tents add to the charm of browsing for unique items. This market has had some controversy as it progressed over time because some of its property was once a cemetery, a vegetable market, wholesale fruit mart and a livestock market. If you are staying in Melbourne for some time and preparing your own meals, you can't do better than to get your meat and produce at the Queen Victoria Market.

There is also the Chapel Street Bazaar with 70 stalls

that have a large stock of second-hand items, cameras, jewelry, toys, clothes, hats and chinaware. If that doesn't satisfy you, just move on to The People's Market, The Flea Market, Markets Melbourne, St. Kilda Market or the Caribbean Gardens Market. There are dozens more of these markets so if you wanted to visit them all, you had better think about moving to Melbourne.

The Caribbean Gardens Market interested me as I wondered why in Australia, with its hot weather during its summer months and warm weather during its winter months they would be indulging in Caribbean lifestyles. The market and its gardens are a fascinating place to visit. It has about 1,000 stalls selling the greatest selection of items outside of the Caribbean countries that we have visited in the past. The fruit and vegetables look delicious. The antique furniture, pottery, paintings, fabrics and a multitude of other items will temps you to spend some money there.

All good things must end, and it was time to leave Melbourne and catch a flight to another part of the intriguing Australian continent. We won't ever forget our wonderful and exciting ride on Puffing Billy.

CHAPTER 7

THE BIG DRIP

Drip, drip, drip!

I rolled over in bed trying to get to sleep.

Drip, drip, drip!

It was a constant dripping sound all night long, and it kept me from going to sleep.

A couple of times Lillian said to me, " Pretend you don't hear it."

How would I pretend that I didn't hear those drops of water hitting the bottom of the basin when they landed like a 10-ton building block dropping from the sky and hitting the ground? Or like a jetliner crashing into the face of Mount Everest?

Of course, everyone knows Everest is the highest mountain in the world. It is 8.9 km above sea level. If you are measuring in miles, it's about 5.5. It is in the Himalaya mountain range on the frontiers of Nepal and Tibet. Repeating all of this information in my head didn't stop the dripping and it didn't get me to sleep.

Drip, drip, drip!

I even tried naming all the mountains I could think of with the hope of getting so tired that I would drop off to sleep. Let's see, there's Mount Elbrus, the highest mountain in Europe; Mount Etna, one of the world's famous volcanoes that stretches high into the air; Mount Fiji, the highest mountain in Japan; Mount Kenya, the second highest mountain in Africa located in Kenya where we spent several weeks investigating; and Mount Kilimanjaro, Africa's highest mountain at 19,340 feet (5,895 metres) in Tanzania.

Drip, drip, drip!

I could not get to sleep with the tap dripping water into that basin in our hotel room in Port-of-Spain, Trinidad. This was some kind of torture like the FBI or the CIA used in their waterboarding technique.

Counting sheep had no effect on my sleepless condition. Counting water droplets didn't put me under either, as it just became a great annoyance. I went to bed at 2:00 a.m. and our wake up call was for 6:00 a.m. I needed every bit of shuteye that I could muster. I just had a very unpleasant day and the next one was going to be eventful. Lillian, on the other hand, could sleep through the fireworks of the American Fourth of July. Once in bed, she was sound asleep. It was only water dripping in the bathroom, but it could have been the roar of Niagara Falls and it wouldn't have made any difference to Lillian. She could sleep lying down, sitting up, or even standing. I could hear a wristwatch tick from across the room in the middle of the night.

Drip, drip, drip!

What were we doing in this hotel in Trinidad? Well, we were not there by choice. It's a long story, and since I can't sleep, I'll keep you up too with this adventure of ours that had gone a bit wacky.

Trinidad and Tobago are two islands that make up one country, simply known as the Republic of Trinidad and Tobago. These islands can be found on the southeast side of the Caribbean Sea. They have the warm blue waters of the Caribbean Sea on one side and the cool waters of the Atlantic Ocean lapping their shores on the east coast. A good baseball player could hit a homerun that would carry from Trinidad's southwest tip of the island across the body of water called the Serpent's Mouth and the ball would land in Venezuela in South America.

We planned to spend Christmas in Tobago and New Years in Trinidad and enjoy the islands for about 15 days. We flew from Toronto to Trinidad's Port-of-Spain on a large jet and then by a small propeller-driven aircraft, hopped over the 70 miles to Scarborough, Tobago. Besides planning to enjoy the tropical islands as a break to the Canadian winter, I had some Christmas presents to deliver to a native family in Tobago.

My good friend Cecil Louie Jr., a young man that I worked with during my years with the Niagara Escarpment Commission, was born in Tobago and his parents and several family members still lived there.

Cecil's father, Cecil Louie Sr. made sure that all eight of his children left the island to get a university education. Some went to England, some to the United States, and Cecil Jr. went to the University of Toronto in Canada.

It didn't take long after Cecil and I met for us to become good friends. Cecil was a planner with the Commission and I was the commission's executive secretary and responsible for information services. When Cecil found out that Lillian and I were going to his childhood home of Tobago, he was delighted and asked if we could take some Christmas presents to his family. Cecil married a girl that he met in Toronto and the two of them had been to Tobago a couple of times for short vacations since the marriage.

His wife would love to move there to enjoy the sun and warm weather, but Cecil said he was accustomed to the efficient service provided by living in Toronto over the laidback and slow-paced life of the island. The total population of both islands reaches about 1.4 million.

Christopher Columbus discovered Trinidad in 1498 and claimed it for Spain. He found friendly Arawak and Carib Indians inhabiting the island. In 1592, the British discovered Tobago and 40 years later the Dutch moved in to settle some parts of that island.

We stayed at a beautiful old sugar mill plantation. The beach was across the road and over the hill but the buildings and great pool made up for the inconvenience of getting to the ocean.
The rich, green golf course sprinkled with palm trees and other colourful shrubbery created a paradise for

vacationers. Most days Lillian and I played golf, although some days she just drove the cart and I did all of the swinging. Nearly every day it would pour rain for about 10 or 15 minutes and although the golf cart had a roof, mainly to protect us from the sun, it also kept the heavy rain off of us. Lillian would just wheel in under a clump of palms and we would sit there for a few minutes, enough time to talk, and then the rain would stop and we continued on with our game. It was so hot that the fairways dried almost immediately.

I had the longest shots of my life on that Tobago golf course. When I hit the ball I thought it had wings as it carried hundreds of feet down the fairway. I thought I improved my game so much that I was ready to turn professional. Reality struck when I talked with some of the attendants at the pro shop. They told me that the extremely hot air currents that flow over Tobago will carry anything you put up in the air like a baseball, kite or even a golf ball. Your golf ball will go twice as far in Tobago as back in Canada. That ended my dream of every becoming a pro. Phooey!

One of the real pleasures of staying at the old sugar plantation was that for several days around Christmas, the management arranged to have school children brought to the resort to sing Christmas carols. If you haven't heard Silent Night sung to a West Indian syncopated calypso beat, then you haven't heard real Christmas music.

I called Cecil's family to make arrangements to deliver the Christmas presents that we brought from Canada.

Cecil let his father know that we were coming to Tobago and they invited us to dinner at their home outside of Scarborough.

Cecil Sr. was the clerk of the borough and a highly respected man in the community. He had an insurance agency, and until tragedy struck a few months before we arrived, he owned a motel that was destroyed by fire.

We arrived for dinner at a very large house on a beautifully landscaped lot with mature trees and colourful plants decorating the lush green lawn. We were made to feel like we were a part of the family with a wonderful welcome. There was a large gathering of people to greet us. There were more relatives and extended family members than you could count. It was like a family reunion. They all came to meet Cecil Jr.'s friends from Canada.

The main floor of the big house had no interior walls. It was just one gigantic room. Kitchen, dining and living quarters took up the whole lower level of this house. There was no glass in some of the windows because it was summer time all year round. In what was likely the living room, a very interesting homemade manger scene was set up by turning a couple chairs over to make the manger. They placed miniature animals around the manger that held baby Jesus. The Louies are faithful Catholics.

Under the supervision of Mrs. Louie, there was enough food prepared to feed an army. It was somewhat embarrassing for Lillian and I when we found out that they prepared American dishes, as well as Caribbean food, in case we didn't like their food. Let me tell you, we preferred the local food. It was delicious. I drank several glasses of a pink juice that tasted oh-so good. Mrs. Louie said to look out the window at the big tree in the yard, the one with the pink flowers.

"The flowers on that tree are used in the making of that sorel drink that you like," Mrs. Louis said. She continued, "And the greens that you are eating come from the leaves of that tree."

That is real living on the island of Tobago.

We stopped back another day to say goodbye to Mr. and Mrs. Louie and to thank them for having us to their home and making us feel like part of their family.

The next day the hotel van took us to the airport for our return flight to Trinidad. Really, I don't think that you could call it an airport, more like an airstrip with a palm leaf roof for the terminal. The terminal was the size of the average bedroom in a house. There were no chairs to sit on, just a counter.

Descending from the van I picked up the two suitcases while Lillian took hold of both carry-ons. As I entered the little shack, a suitcase in each hand, the man in charge (the only man there) rather barked at me.

"Leave the bags outside," growled the oversized attendant as he disappeared out the back door of the shack.

I turned and exited, parking the two bags just outside

the door. Lillian asked me what I was doing as she wondered if we were not able to fly. I explained that this is the baggage drop-off at the Tobago airstrip.

There was an old wooden bench outside the shack and Lillian sat on it. I decided to stand ready for orders from the attendant. All of a sudden the attendant reappeared from the back of the shack, grabbed our luggage and disappeared around the corner of the building. By this time there were three other pieces of luggage sitting there outside the shack. I think Lillian was quite enjoying this mysterious "Terminal One" single-man staff.

I was curious, so I took a few steps around the end of the shack. I saw all five bags piled on a little cart. I looked up and down the narrow airstrip that wasn't really very long. It would only accommodate small planes. Part way down the strip and off to the left was a small aircraft sitting in about three feet of grass. It appeared to have been there for some time. Further down the strip there was another small plane sitting on its belly. Somehow it lost its wheels. Several of its little windows were knocked out and it looked like a lonely forgotten throwaway.

I returned to where Lillian was waiting at the front of the shack. The other three passengers were quietly waiting under a big tree a short distance away. It appeared that two of the men were travelling together but the third fellow was all by himself.

Just then we heard the roar of a plane engine somewhere in the sky. Finally, there is was, floating down from the blue sky above. When the wheels hit the paved airstrip, they bounced a couple of times as the plane carried on down the runway until it cruised to a stop near the end of the pavement. Turning, it headed back along the strip and stopped about 50 feet directly behind the shack. At this point, our one-man ground crew grabbed the handle of the cart and at a slower than slow speed pulled the cart with the five suitcases on it out to the airplane.

The engine of the plane chugged a couple of times, sputtered a bit, and then went completely dead. The pilot swung his little door open and hopped out to meet the fellow with the luggage. An animated conversation took place. Now with arms waving, a little shouting which was unintelligible and a couple of hard stomps with a foot to the ground by each combatant, it was a strange sight. It looked like a couple of peacocks doing a mating dance.

The general manager of "Terminal One" lifted the five pieces of luggage into the back of the aircraft. The pilot kept throwing up his arms like a man in desperation before attempting to go over Niagara Falls. The baggage attendant turned and pushed the empty cart back toward the shack. The pilot opened his door and climbed in behind all those little round gages on the instrument panel. That little plane groaned, it shook, it belched before some black smoke shot out of its exhaust pipe.

All was silent for a moment and then the little plane roared like a lion as the propeller turned over a few times. Suddenly there were flashes of fire shooting out of the exhaust pipe like the flames of a fire-breathing dragon. Finally the propeller was spinning and the plane moved ahead a short distance. The plane stopped, turned sharply around and headed down the runway. It was gaining speed and before you knew it, the wheels were off the ground and the plane was airborne. It was back in the rich blue sky above us. It was soon just a speck in the heavens and then it was gone.

Stunned, we stood there and watched that little plane take off with our luggage aboard. Talk about losing your bags, that hijacking little airplane just stole ours.

I rushed into the little shack that was pretending to be an air terminal, and I'm afraid using a louder voice than usual, informed the attendant that the plane had taken off without us but carried away our suitcases.

By this time the other candidates for the proposed flight back to Trinidad had crowded into the little shack and were all trying to talk at once.

"Calm down, calm down," said the attendant, "another plane will be here shortly to take you over the water."

I asked why the plane left with our luggage but didn't take us along as well.

"The plane that just took off was having engine trouble and it was not safe to fly onboard," he said. "In case it doesn't make it across the sea, we didn't want any passengers on it."

I suggested if the plane wasn't safe for us, it wasn't safe for the pilot either.

"Oh," he said. "If the plane goes down, Martin is a good swimmer."

I hoped that he was just joking about the pilot. And what about our suitcases?

The attendant, who by now we realized wore several hats in operating this airfield, explained that he didn't have any facilities to fix airplanes. It was just a strip where planes landed and departed from. Any planes with mechanical problems must go back to Trinidad for repairs. That probably answered my earlier curiosities about the two old planes sitting off the edge of the runway. They couldn't make it back to Trinidad.

He explained that another plane was on its way to Tobago from Trinidad to take us back to the big island. About 40 minutes later, our ride arrived. All five of us climbed on board for an uneventful flight over the Caribbean Sea to land safely in Trinidad.

Our week in Trinidad at the Hilton Trinidad and Conference Centre Hotel was enjoyable. It was located on Lady Young Road on a beautifully landscaped property on the side of a very steep hill. The locals called it a mountain. We entered on the top floor at the main desk. A bellhop assisted us with the luggage and took us on the elevator down about four floors to our room. There were several floors still below us. At first it seemed a bit strange that each time we wanted to leave our room we had to press 'up' on the elevator. When we wanted to go out of the hotel we had to go up to the lobby.

The hotel, hanging on the side of the 'mountain', provided us with a tremendous view of Queen's Park Savannah, a large open space park of about 200 acres of grass and recreation facilities that had a small river running through it. There are soccer fields, cricket grounds and racetracks that compliment the open space. We could see the built-up city stretching beyond it. And further to the west was the Caribbean Sea.

We enjoyed our stay at this hotel, especially New Year's Eve. A very romantic and exquisitely-decorated small dining room at the top of the building that held only about 20 tables was the location for our last celebration of the year. We made the reservation about six months in advance. That night, everything was 10-star service. The Hilton flew in a world-class singer from Israel named Ali Kazan just to entertain us for the evening. She was marvelous.

A couple of days later we received a telephone call from two of the cousins we had met at the Louie family dinner. They had just arrived from Tobago to attend the horse races that day and invited us to join them at the track. We did, and had a wonderful time with our new friends.

On another day, we explored the downtown area of Port-of-Spain. We visited a few hotels as we usually do when visiting new places. We rate them and compare them so if we ever return to that city, we know the best places to stay. Upon exiting the Holiday Hotel, I told Lillian to make a note that we would never spend a night in that place. It didn't even rate on a scale of one to 10. I gave it a minus.

We thought our adventure time in Trinidad and Tobago had come to an end. We were ready to go home. We packed our bags and had a good night's sleep at the Trinidad Hilton. Tomorrow's journey would take us back home to Canada. The next morning we took about a 45-minute taxi ride to the airport. Our international flight was to leave at 11 a.m. We didn't bother to have any lunch, as we were to have lunch on the plane. There was no trouble going through customs and immigration, as they want you to take all kinds of purchased items out of the country as long as you leave your dollars behind.

We walked across the tarmac and climbed the stairs to the waiting jet. We got comfortable in our assigned seats, tightened our seatbelts and were ready to go. We were, but the airline wasn't.

We sat there for quite some time until a passenger asked a flight attendant about the delay that was preventing us from taking off.

"You see sir," the young woman said, "the captain is having problems with the electrical system and as you may have noticed, it is getting quite warm in here because the air conditioning isn't working."

We sat on the plane for nearly four hours, without food and without air conditioning. Some of the passengers asked if they could disembark but were told they couldn't because we had cleared immigration. Finally the pilot announced that we were ready to take off.

Fasten your seatbelts. Again!

We taxied out to the runway and all the way down to the end of it. The plane turned about, roared its engines and down the runway we headed, gathering speed as we passed by the terminal. Then suddenly a screeching sound accompanied by a few jerks and the plane practically stood on its nose as we stopped dead, right at the end of the runway.

"What's next?" Lillian exclaimed, as she sat looking out of the plane's window that was just ahead of the wing. I told her I didn't have the foggiest idea, but I guess it would have been faster to take a hot air balloon to go home rather than an airplane out of Trinidad and Tobago.

One of the flight attendants came through the cabin to check if all the passengers were alright after the sudden jolt from stopping so suddenly.

"This is the captain speaking," roared a loud voice over the PA system. "A cargo door sprung open and we had to stop in a hurry. I'm sorry about that so we will have to turn around and go back to get it fixed."

He certainly was right. The plane turned around and taxied back down the runway, then crossed the tarmac and stopped at the same place we had parked for hours before we ventured out onto the runway the first time. It took nearly three hours to fix the baggage compartment door. Remember Cecil Louie Jr.? He said he wanted to remain living in Toronto where things happened instantly. He didn't want to move back to the islands where it takes forever to get things done.

It was now dark outside and we still hadn't eaten. My stomach thought I was fasting for some kind of religious purpose. The flight attendant said she couldn't serve us until we got into the air.

"Ladies and gentleman," said the captain. "We are ready to take another run at it so we are heading out to the runway."

Lillian leaned over to me and said, "Don't get your hopes up."

It was the same old routine: taxi down to the end of the runway, turn the aircraft around, roar the engines and full throttle ahead down the runway. This time I felt a liftoff and then heard the wheels pull back up into the undercarriage and I knew we were in the air.

We were in the air for 10 minutes when I leaned over to Lillian and quietly whispered that I thought the plane was turning around.

"I'm too tired for any humour right now," she said. I told her I wasn't kidding and the plane had definitely turned around. Just then, the captain's voice came over the PA system again.

"Our navigational system is not functioning and it is necessary to turn around and go back to the airport," he said. "If we continued on over the Atlantic we could lose our way without this system."

He informed us that he had dropped to a fairly low altitude so that he could see lights from buildings along the shoreline and he was attempting to follow the lights back to the airport.

"Say no more," chirped Lillian. "We are going to spend the rest of our lives in Trinidad."

After landing at the airport the passengers were herded into the arrival room for a customs and immigration check. I thought it was very foolish because we had never really left the country other than to go up into the air and back down again. We still had to show our passports and answer questions like "are you bringing anything into the country?" and "how long do you intend to stay?"

You must be polite and patient when dealing with customs and immigration people. They always get the last word. I really wanted to say that I was only going to stay in the country long enough to get something to eat as I hadn't eaten all day and I was starving. After all, most countries accept starving people, don't they?

After a grueling time getting back into Trinidad, a country we had really never left, the airline provided the passengers with a bus to take us into Port-of-Spain to spend the remainder of the night at a hotel they were providing free to us. Generous of them, eh?

It was after midnight when we arrived at the hotel. Maybe you've guessed which one it was by now. That

Holiday Hotel that I rated minus on the chart. It was the hotel that I told Lillian we would never stay in. This was the airline's choice. The airline asked the night clerk to prepare some sandwiches for the passengers but the food was so bad that most of us couldn't eat it. Let's just get to bed and get some much-needed sleep. We had to be back at the airport by 8 a.m.

Drip, drip, drip!

This is how the whole story started. I really never got any sleep that night.

Drip, drip, drip!

The bathroom tap just kept going like that rabbit with the batteries in it. Before I knew it, the telephone rang with our wakeup call and to remind us that the bus would be there soon to take us back to the airport.

You guessed it – back through customs and immigration again. They must have thought that we did a lot of flying in and out of Trinidad. We boarded a plane that had arrived earlier that morning. It was serviced and ready to go, unlike the one we attempted to fly out on the previous day. This flight, however, was not a direct one to Toronto. We stopped in Kingston, Jamaica to pick up more passengers.

When we arrived at Toronto Pearson Airport, there was another surprise waiting for us – snow. Lots and lots of snow covered the runways in Toronto. After circling around Toronto about five time in the air, the pilot was allowed to land his aircraft. Once on the ground, we had to wait at the end of the runway for over an hour while snowplows worked feverishly to clear a space at the gate so that our plane could taxi in and passengers could deplane.

Home at last!

Fly with me, only if you are looking for something out of the ordinary.

CHAPTER 8

THE NEXT SEAT

How often have you sat in a seat on an airplane and had the seat beside you empty? This has happened to me on several flights and gives one a little extra space. It usually is a little quieter and more restful on the flight, too.

On one 12-hour flight that Lillian and I had from Amsterdam in the Netherlands to Nairobi, Kenya, in the heart of Africa, I could choose just about any seat on the giant Boeing 747. The crew on this KLM flight outnumbered the 12 passengers on board. The plane's capacity was 524. The reason for the large aircraft going to Nairobi was to pick up some of the two thousand people waiting at the airport. They were attempting to flee the country as 1,000 people were murdered in the capital city over the course of the last month. Most of the people who were killed had their heads removed. Yes, chopped off. That is another story.

Sometimes I have had the most delightful and gracious person sitting next to me. I once had the head of the Ministry of Education in Bermuda sit next to me and I helped him write a speech that he had to give that same night after landing in Bermuda. I have written many speeches for cabinet ministers when I worked at Queen's Park in Toronto.

Lillian once had a very enjoyable flight home from Barbados sitting in first class next to the country's head of electricity for the island. The conversation with the commissioner was most enlightening as they flew from Bridgetown to Toronto. On that same flight, just two rows ahead, was the Right Honourable John Diefenbaker, Prime Minister of Canada.

Though the best, the very best conversation with a fellow passenger sitting next to me occurred on a flight from Toronto to Los Angeles, Lillian and I were on our way to Australia via California and the South Pacific Island of Moorea. We made a stop on the North Island of New Zealand and finally arrived in Sydney, Australia. We took the long route, as I planned to do some stories on the tropical island of Moorea. On this island, I met with the trainers at Dolphin Quest and they put some of the dolphins through a drill to show me how they are trained.

When flying, I usually spend most of my time reading, but on our initial leg of this trip – that stretch from Toronto to L.A. – I didn't read a word. I had a conversation with my newfound friend, Lowell De Mond and his wife Marion, who were heading directly to New Zealand after switching planes in Los Angeles. I can honestly say that Lowell was one of the most interesting people I've ever met. This couple was from the Canadian Maritimes and this alone makes for an interesting conversation. As it turned out, there was a lot more to the conversation when Lowell added in his great storytelling soaked in humour. This all happened more than a decade ago and I still find myself laughing at some of the stories he told me. Lowell was not a comedian, but he was surely the best storyteller in the country.

Lowell R. DeMond of Bridgewater, Nova Scotia is a retired school principal. It would have been fun to be a student at his school. He is alive and full of energy, wanting the best for his students and the land and water where they live. An avid fisherman from the time he was old enough to hold a fishing pole, he would go fishing in the mornings before he went to school as a teacher. That is dedication to the sport.

When Lowell was a boy attending elementary school, he even went fishing on the way to school in the early morning. Lunch was an hour and fifteen minutes long, giving Lowell and some of his buddies plenty of time to run across the road that separated the school from the Medway River and do a little noon hour fishing.

One of the funny stories he told me was about a farm neighbor by the name of Mr. Fancy. Lowell promised to go fishing with Mr. Fancy and went over to his house early one morning to join him and his two sons, Donnie and Bob. Ethel, who is Mr. Fancy's wife, had boiled some corn on the cob and placed it in Mr. Fancy's backpack. Without knowing, Mr. Fancy put his arms through the straps of the backpack and then tied the straps together across his chest. The pack was very secure.

All of a sudden Mr. Fancy began to scream and jump around all over the kitchen. He kept yelling that he was on fire or at least burning to death. He shouted at Ethel, asking what was in the backpack. "Only hot corn," she replied.

Poor Mr. Fancy. He couldn't get the backpack off because he'd tied the straps so tightly together. He kept jumping up and down and running around the house like a chicken with its head cut off. He knocked over some furniture and when he turned over a big chair where the cat was sleeping, the cat screamed and jumped on the window curtain. The cat didn't like the commotion one bit and climbed up the curtain to sit on the curtain rod across the top of the window. All this time Mr. Fancy was screaming and yelling that he was burning to death. Ethel finally managed to get the backpack off her husband and covered the bright red spots on his back with butter.

Mr. Fancy settled down, Donnie and Bob located their fishing gear and were ready to go. But there's more to the boys' fishing trip that morning. There is the bull pulling an ox cart that took the so-called fishermen to the river. What do you do with a wild bull?

As Lowell was telling me all of these outlandish things, there was no time for me to open one of my books, all I could do was laugh. The best part about Lowell's stories is that this storytelling genius compiled them into a book called *Hooked!* There are 23 short fishing stories in this marvelous book. A couple of months after meeting Lowell and his wife on that Air Canada flight, he sent me a copy of his book. I've read *Hooked!* more times than I can count and I'd highly recommend looking up Lowell R. DeMond on your favorite online bookseller's site to pick up your own copy.

Many of his stories that he told me while sitting in the next seat on that Air Canada flight at 30,000 feet heading to LAX were better than any comedy show on television. I particularly liked the story about old Gert and his disregard for the law prohibiting the starting of salmon fishing on the LeHave River before 6:00 a.m. What is time to an old dodger?

Gert, according to Lowell, would get to the river well before the bewitching hour of six in the morning and push off his boat, heading for the pool he knew had salmon in it. Eighty-plus-year old Gert was doing what he liked best in life – fishing. Really, did it matter what time of day or night it was as long as this old man enjoyed fishing and wasn't hurting anyone else? It was just a few minutes before six when two fishing officers showed up and yelled at Gert that he was breaking the law by fishing before the legal hour. Gert pulled his line out of the water and apologized to the officers, claiming he didn't know the exact time. This time, he got away without a ticket.

Two days later, Gert was back at it again in the same spot in the river, right by the pool where the best salmon could be caught. He was standing in the small boat waving his rod around like a band conductor with his baton. The fly on the end of the line could be seen going in one direction and then in the other. There were about six minutes left before the legal hours began. Lowell told me the same two officers, called "fun spoilers" by some of the anglers, appeared on the riverbank. Gert knew that this time they would not be as lenient and he would be charged for fishing before 6:00 a.m. on the LaHave River. A harsh treatment for the old-timer who spent most of his life fishing.

Old Gert appeared in court a few days later. The court audience was bigger that day than the opening day of fishing season. Every fisherman within miles showed up to witness old Gert pleading not guilty to the charge. He bravely defended himself in court before the judge.

That old fisherman, turned lawyer for the day, proceeded to inform the judge of the difference between flies used for trout fishing. I don't know how much the judge knew about trout fishing, but as Lowell explained to me, old Gert kept talking about dry flies and wet flies. He claimed not to have started fishing before the 6:00 a.m. official opening time. Gert said he was only drying out his wet flies before the legal start time to fish in the LeHave.

The judge that day was in a sympathetic mood toward the old man. It was probably the best fishing story of a defense that he'd heard in a long time. It certainly was a complicated one that Lowell tried explaining to a non-fisherman like me. The judge dismissed the charge against Gert, warning him to never appear in his courtroom again or he would face serious consequences.

The judge was hooked, and so was I.

Lowell is a pretty unique guy. Who else would travel all the way from Nova Scotia to Stratford, Ontario on his honeymoon, just to take his new bride to see a play by William Shakespeare? And after the play, Lowell took

Marion to see Niagara Falls.

Throughout his life, Lowell DeMond has fought for clean water in our rivers to protect the fish stock. He carried his fight to offshore waters where fish pens have caused needless problems

The following is an excerpt from one of Lowell's letters for the editor of a Maritimes newspaper:

"Since the wild Atlantic salmon have almost disappeared, and with this news of the dying aquaculture salmon, it's easy to understand why the LaHave River Salmon Association has opted for roast beef at its annual dinner and auction this coming Saturday night."

Lowell has been greatly involved in the LaHave River Salmon Association for many years. He told me that the juvenile fish are leaving our rivers and going to the ocean, but the adult fish are not coming back, making it a marine problem. Running into the Bay of Fundy are 32 rivers, all of which had runs of Atlantic salmon. At the present time, many have lost their runs and others are listed as endangered.

His fight to save the fish and maintain clean waters in our rivers has been a lifelong crusade. From Lowell's schoolboy days to his retirement from his principal's duties, he has kept his standards high.

There were so many other stories Lowell told me on that flight, just too numerous to include here. I was thinking that if I have to sit next to someone on an airplane, I would pick another storyteller like Lowell DeMond. In all of his fight for right, he's never lost his sense of humour.

FLY WITH ME

Above, the Southern Fueguean Railway outside and inside the engine. Lillian (top right) is sitting in a cold, unheated train car.

The railway was built by prisoners. One of the present day workers (middle) is dressed in an old prison uniform.

In the bottom photo, Walter is pictured with a crew member of the MS Explorer.

WALTER W. GOWING

Above: Puffing Billy, the historic steam engine in Australia.

Below: Walter driving the Indian Pacific as it leaves Adelaide for Perth, Australia. It travels the longest straight rail line in the world. Don't worry – Walter didn't get a speeding ticket on this run.

PART THREE

THE OUTBACK

CHAPTER 9

GHOST TOWNS

A long flight or a slow ship's cruise to a fantastic location to board a train is often well worth the trip. While we are thinking of trains, I am reminded of the Indian Pacific train operated by the Great Southern Railway that took Lillian and I across the continent of Australia from Sydney to Perth, accommodating us in the Royal Suite. It is the longest straight stretch of rail in the world. I even had the opportunity to be up front in the locomotive after a stop at Adelaide. I got to drive the train in return for taking the engineer's picture, which he hoped would be included in a newspaper story I was doing on crossing Australia by train.

It was some time after leaving Adelaide on our way west that we reached the once-thriving community of Cook. Today, Cook is a ghost town in the middle of the desert outback. It is located about 2,700 km west of Sydney and was once a booming settlement of 100 people. With the introduction of diesel trains, Cook lost its importance as a train stop to take on water and wood for the old steam locomotives. Now only three people live there and their occupation is selling souvenirs to the twice-a-week passenger train that stops for tourism purposes.

Lillian and I have visited ghost towns before. Well, at

least the sites where real towns once existed. In North America one of the best ghost town adventures is located in the mountains, west of Denver and Colorado Springs. We once got lost in these mountains and it can be quite frightening. In the daylight hours it can be warm and comfortable, but when darkness covers the tops of these mountains – look out, it can get very cold.

The Continental Divide runs just west of Colorado Springs. This unique line with its highest mountaintops on the continent controls whether the rivers that come out of the mountains flow east or west. Many of the mountain peaks in this area surpass the 14,000-foot level. Mt. Antera reaches 14,269 feet while Mt. Harvard climbs to 14,420 feet, and the neighbouring Mt. Elbert tops at 14,433 feet.

There are some fascinating places in and around Cripple Creek and Victor. Many small towns came into existence after gold was discovered in 1858 in Colorado. Boom! Mining towns blossomed all over the mountains, especially if a rail line was nearby. In the olden days, trains were the lifeblood of an emerging nation. When the railroad stopped running or was moved to a different location, the small towns it originally served usually died. Nothing was left but a ghost town.

One of the great experiences in Colorado's mountains was riding on a narrow gauge railroad that passed dozens of former gold mines. Travelling this route on the Cripple Creek & Victor Narrow Gauge Railroad is a thrill for train lovers. The steam locomotive and its near-dozen old coaches were pulled by a puffing and snorting 15-ton iron horse of the 0-4-0 type that was typical of the early days when steam engines were regularly used to win the west.

We rolled by the remnants of old worked-out mines and the rusty equipment abandoned when the mine was no longer profitable. A number of the long-deserted mines had a weather-beaten rustic old post protruding from the crust of the earth. Nailed on the post would be a piece of timber with the name of the former working mine. Some of the names included *Gold King Mine, Moon Anchor Mine, Anchoria-Leland Mine,* and *Ducking Mine.* It was interesting to see a female touch among the mines when we spotted the sign for the *Mary McKinney Mine.*

It was intriguing to see small individual mines that were dug by pick and shovel, sometimes a one-man operation that had long been given up because of the lack of gold. It is estimated that during the working days of the mines in Colorado, over $800 million worth of gold was extracted. I wondered if I left the train and picked up a shovel, would I find gold if I started to dig down a little further? Lillian warned me to be careful of gold fever because it can be addictive like gambling.

This rail line was unusual because after an hour's journey we got off in a small town that still had a working casino. I couldn't find anything else or anyone working in the town. Once a couple of busy bordellos were across the street from the casino but they now appeared to be closed. Maybe it is because the girls sleep in the daytime and ply their trade at night. The surprise was getting back on the train for the return trip and finding that the train had to back up the entire way. There was no facility at the station to turn the engine around so it had to go in reverse the whole way home. Here were about 10 old wooden coaches connected to a steam engine, moving backwards at about the same speed we went forward on the way into the mountains. It was impossible for the engineer in the locomotive at the rear of the train to see what was in front of us as we rambled down the track. What if someone were on the track or a tree had fallen across the rails? The engineer would never know until he hit it.

Back in Australia, where the train manager on Australia's Indian Pacific made it very clear that Cook was just a one-hour stop. It would be a great opportunity for us to visit an unbelievable ghost town in the middle of South Australia. I checked my wristwatch, the one Lillian gave to me for my birthday about five decades ago. I can't remember the year on February 10, although the boys were in strollers with us at Disneyland in California. It was probably 1962 or 1963. The watch had a gold Mickey Mouse on its face. It has kept perfect time now for more than half a century. It's a real treasure with Swiss works and I wear it every day. Oh yes, the time in Cook. It was 10:00 a.m. on a Saturday morning.

There was a warning to passengers getting off the train in Cook. The train manager cautioned everyone to be back on board the train before it left the station. He emphasized that there were only two westbound trains a week running from Sydney to Perth, and it's no picnic sleeping on the desert sand at night with wild hungry dingoes roaming about.

The train manager was right; shortly after we boarded the train following our ghost town visit, we looked out the window as the train pulled away from the outback post, and sure enough, a sandy-coloured sleek-looking Australian wild dog strutted alongside the train for about a kilometre. Dingoes are usually a yellow-ginger colour, although I've seen a couple of black and tan ones. They often live in packs so that they can share the raising of the pups. These animals can be very dangerous. They will kill anything from a small mouse to a large kangaroo. There have been numerous reports that dingoes attacked and made off with small native children. Some African countries have the extremely vicious and nasty hyenas, while Australia has its equally bad dingoes.

During our stop in Cook, we visited the empty town that had about a dozen buildings stretched out along its main street. A couple of stores were just sitting there, waiting for customers. The stores, of course, had no merchandise. Stores with counters and shelves all empty and ready to be stocked. They were a little dusty with no one around to care for them after the residents evacuated. Not a clerk was in sight; the place was deserted.

Lillian and I looked through the windows of the small school. All the desks were in place and waiting for students to take their seats. There were no children living in Cook anymore. The schoolhouse sat there in an era of ghostly silence, wondering whatever happened to the happy children who sang, played, and learned in its classroom. I'm not even sure there were any ghosts living in this abandoned town.

We looked at a row of empty bungalows sitting

quietly and awaiting their inhabitants who would never return. We visited the local hospital at the other end of the street. It looked as though all of the staff and patients were taking the day off. Inside the building, the rooms of the small hospital looked liked they were ready to accept new patients at any moment. Against the outside walls on one side of the hospital building was the only evidence of neglect as the drifting sand was accumulating up the wall, grasping at the windowsills.

Only a stone's throw away sat an empty in-ground cement swimming pool. The chrome ladders still in place but no one to climb up or down them. When I say empty, I mean without water. The pool was full, or nearly full of drifting sand. Lillian suggested it would made a great sandbox for children. Being in the middle of the sometimes cruel, treeless Nullarbor Plain produced some harsh living conditions for the residents. Cook's experience is of the past, with no future for the community on the horizon.

And finally, there before us was the Cook Golf Club with a large sign stressed that "All Visitors Welcome" and inviting us to play. The sign said the sand green fees were two dollars for the 9-hole course and the hours were from 11:00 a.m. to 11:00 p.m. I'm afraid you would need florescent balls and a flashlight even if you thought about playing late into the evening. There was no grass. It was just one giant-sized sand trap. Oh, how I wished I brought my golf clubs with me! Just then, the train whistle blew and it was time to leave the little ghost town of Cook.

The 20-car train of the Indian Pacific, with its

impressive emblem showing the wedge-tailed eagle – the largest eagle in Australia – gives the traveller the confidence of a safe and secure journey. Its gigantic wingspan symbolizes the accomplishment of spanning the island continent by the Indian Pacific Railway.

Leaving Cook, the train continued on its westward journey over the longest stretch of straight rail tracks in the world – 478 km. In the early years of the 20th century, different areas of the country had their own railways with a mishmash of rail lines from narrow gauge to broad gauge rails. It was not until 1969 that a single continuous railway line (4,352 km) was operating from the Pacific Ocean to the Indian Ocean. There is where the Indian Pacific railway got its name and became one of the largest continuous rail journeys in the world.

Early one morning I awoke when the Indian Pacific stopped in the middle of nowhere. I quickly dressed and hurried down the train's narrow corridor to the open door at the end of the coach. Descending the steep steps, I met the train manager standing on the ground.

"What's going on?" I asked, hoping it wasn't a mechanical failure. We already experienced a three-hour delay in Adelaide while an air conditioning unit in one of the front cars was repaired. It can get very hot crossing the desert without air conditioning in a train coach.

"Only some darn old sleeping camels have stopped us," the manager replied.

"What do you mean sleeping camels?" I fired back as

the two of us began to walk towards the front of the train. Our coach was in the middle of a very long line of train cars.

"Oh, this happens once in awhile," the congenial manager said. Down Under they call the train conductors "train managers." He spent a few hours in our large compartment telling us a lot of great history about the railway and Australia's outback.

As we approached the engine at the front end of the train, I couldn't believe my own eyes. There before us were four enormous camels sleeping on the railway track. As I checked out one of the camels lying there, its large pads on its hind feet were clearly visible, along with its two toes on each hoof stocking out over one side of the rails, while its head and neck were comfortably hanging over the opposite rail on the track bed. These camels were taking over the railway track and its bed for their own bed and a good night's sleep.

Really, it was no laughing matter because the camels refused to get up and move. The engineer got a broom from the train's housekeeper and with it began to prod the unmovable beasts with the broomstick. These camels were wild in the outback and could be dangerous. After all, they plied the outback sands long before the railroad was built. The early transportation across the desert in Australia was by camels imported from Africa and the eastern world. After the introduction of planes and trains in Australia, there was no further need for camels and they were simply turned loose to roam on their own.

There now, one camel is up and chased off the tracks.

Now a stubborn second camel is dislodged from the rail right-of-way. The engineer is doing a great job with the broom handle while the train manager is waving his arms. It was a coordinated attack on the drowsy camels. The third camel is on its front knees. Even I got into the act, waving and shouting and carrying on like a crazy Canuck at a Grey Cup game. It looks like the yelling and swinging of arms is going to get the camel up on its feet. Yes, up it gets and staggers off the track. Good, we got three camels off the train tracks and have one more to go. Wait a minute – the first camel decided that he is coming back to reclaim what he thinks is his section of the track.

"Walter!" yelled the train manager. "Don't get too close to that big one! He thinks he owns the track."

It was a standoff between a stubborn camel and stubborn a manager.

"I will be careful," I said, full of confidence. Honestly, I really didn't know what I was doing. After all, I had never fought a herd of camels before in my life.

Both Lillian and I rode camels in Egypt, Tunisia and Morocco. It's like driving a car without a steering wheel. Once in the country of Oman, I visited a camel farm and one of those overzealous long-legged desert thieves stuck his neck over the fence and grabbed my Tilley hat with its big mouth and his constantly chewing teeth. I wouldn't recommend a camel for a pet. And, although I went to a camel market in the United Arab Emirates, I really know very little about these beasts of the sandy desert.

I gathered up some scrub bush that was blown into reach about a train car length from the front end of the locomotive. There I was, just like Sir Lancelot, only without the suit of armor, ready to fight the enemy. I felt like a brave knight of King Arthur's court, ready to protect the poor and the weak, search for the Holy Grail and charge ahead all because of the love of a lady. Swinging that faded grey to brown shrub around and sounding like some Zulus that I once met in South Africa, I made that hissing, spitting, bully of a camel retreat. In the meantime, the engineer prodded the fourth camel off the tracks and it looked like victory was surely ours.

"Good job, mates!" said the train manager. "Everybody on board as we have to make up some lost time."

What an experience! I found these Australian lads to be great guys. We all worked together. Once the camels were removed from the tracks, the engineer climbed back into his locomotive and the train was moving west again.

By the time we were back on track, it was time for breakfast. I stopped by our compartment to shave and wash up, and then Lillian and I took off for the dining car. I really worked up my appetite that morning. It's not every day that one has a cardio workout with four camels before breakfast.

Most people on the train knew nothing about the

camel episode. Some people paid little attention to the few minutes that the train was stopped, while others were still sleeping as the sun rose that morning. Being in the right place at the right time can be very rewarding, eh mate?

WALTER W. GOWING

CHAPTER 10

TRAIN WRECK

There is one more stop along this three-night, four-day rail trip across the expansive continent of Australia that I think has some significance and should be included in this story.

As the Indian Pacific train rolled along heading west across Australia toward Kalgoorlie, a Wild West gold mining town, we passed some small communities like Forrest, Rawlinna and Zanthus. If you really want to escape from civilization but have your newspaper dropped off once a week by a high-speed train roaring by, pick one of these unfamiliar places and take up residence.

Forrest, with a population of 17 living souls, brags about being on the longest stretch of straight rail line in the world. This is not really a big selling point for real estate when you are many, many kilometres from anywhere. This desert community does have a historical claim to fame that dates back to 1929 and runs until 1934.

Forrest has a single landing strip in the desert. It became an overnight stop for Western Australian Airways flying from Perth to Adelaide. A hostel there accommodated the passengers and crew. Unfortunately, with modern jets and diesel locomotives, Forrest was left behind by a fast-moving world that cares little about yesterday.

Continuing west on the Indian Pacific, we passed the community known as Rawlinna. The area receives only about nine inches of rain annually with temperatures of 38 degrees Celcius in the summer months and 19 degrees in the winter. It is a remote spot on the Trans-Australian Railway in the western part of the country. Not far away there is small mine that produces limestone that is used in the gold production process at Kalgoorlie.

Back in the days when the trains were pulled by steam engines, the little stations along the tracks were staffed by railway employees. Rawlinna had a small school for the children of railway workers. You can't purchase gasoline or diesel fuel in Rawlinna. If you need these products, you can get them in Cocklebiddy or Caiguna, about 100 km south of Rawlinna. It's a long way to go to fill up a gas tank, right mate?

In 1967, some of the rail line was washed out in a number of locations in Western Australia. This was caused by a storm that dumped great volumes of water on dry land unprepared for a soak. The storm left the Indian Pacific stranded at Rawlinna. The passengers were facing near-starvation before the crisis was over. Now there was one thing possible for the passengers to pass the time while marooned in the outback: you could write some postcards to friends and family back home. Rawlinna had a post office. Don't shout hurray just yet, because the mail from the Rawlinna Post Office is taken across the country on the Indian Pacific. Remember, you are sitting on the stranded train that is to carry that mail. Oh well, that's outback life.

As our train approached the next little community along the line, I wondered how this place could be any different from the other places that cling to the steel band of rails running through the desert. Passing through Zanthus, 739 km (459 miles) northeast of our final destination, the city of Perth and the port of Freemantle on the Indian Ocean, we were reminded of a major train wreck here on August 18, 1999. The Zanthus made headlines in every newspaper in the nation.

Australia is a big, expansive country. Your neighbor may live hours away from you in the outback. Distance is not an obstacle when an emergency occurs and help is needed. Everyone lends a hand. The Royal Flying Doctor Service is a great example of mercy with wings. It can be a struggle to survive in a land where the elements are not often friendly to humans. It's a land for the hardy and one that requires perseverance.

On that unfortunate day in 1999, an eastbound freight train was on a rail loop that crosses the main east-west line of the Trans-Australian railway running between Perth and Sydney. It was waiting for the westbound Indian Pacific passenger train to pass before looping back onto the main eastbound rail line. The front end of the freight train with its gigantic diesel-fueled engine had not cleared the other track and was sitting there like a brick wall waiting for disaster to strike. The Indian Pacific locomotive and its 19 cars were barreling down on the rail intersection. There was no planned stop at Zanthus and so the engineer kept his train flying across the scrublands of the desert. Although the engineer of the passenger train applied its braking system, records show it was traveling at 27 km/h on impact.

This must have been a terrifying experience for the engineer, knowing that at the last moment he was going to hit the steel freight car in front of him. He had continuously applied the brakes to help save his train and the passengers aboard the Indian Pacific.

It hit the freight train broadside and all 19 of the passenger train's cars were damaged. If you believe in miracles, here's one: not one person was killed in the major collision. There were many people serious injured including passengers and crew. Those people were transported to a remote airstrip at Coonana, about four kilometres (2.5 miles) south of the Trans-Australian Railway line, but some 40 km from Zanthus, which was further back on the line. Coonana is an indigenous community with a population of about 80 natives. From here, the Royal Flying Doctor Service was able to evacuate the injured and fly them to the small hospital at Kalgoorlie. Several flights were necessary for the 21 injured passengers to get help.

Early in our trip the train manager told Lillian and I about the various little communities and especially about Zanthus and the train wreck. Here we were, right at this moment, travelling at a good rate of speed along the very same track used by the doomed train.

We cleared Zanthus and continued rolling along the

steel track on our way to a stop at Kalgoorlie. The train manager sent each first class passenger a notice that he could arrange for a bus to be at the Kalgoorlie station to take us on a tour of Kalgoorlie-Boulder and the Super Pit Gold Mine. The train would be held over at the station for about three hours so we would have enough time to see some interesting sites. Fifteen people responded in a positive way for taking a bus tour of the area. Of course, everyone was hoping to get a gold nugget at the mine. This was only a dream, as none of the workers or visitors get to keep any gold from the mine. Nevertheless, it was a great opportunity for us to see the community and its famous gold mine. We jumped at the chance.

WALTER W. GOWING

CHAPTER 11

OH, THOSE SWINGING DOORS!

Kalgoorlie is a town where the beer flows to the words and tune of Banjo Paterson's Waltzing Matilda. Someone there told me that when this piece of music comes up in a saloon, everyone orders another round of Australian beer. Aussies like their beer. Singing to the music and swashing down jugs of local brew make for a night out in Australia's remote towns. The saloons collect many of the miners when they come off shift to rouse it up a bit before sleeping it off.

The miners hit the saloons with a swashbuckling stride and after a few drinks become noisy, blustering good-natured characters right out of an old Wallace Berry movie. Work hard, drink hard and play hard, then sleep it off before another round of work, drink and play. Those Kalgoorlie saloons really do have swinging doors.

When the train pulled into Kalgoorlie station, the 15 adventurers who signed up for the bus tour were asked to meet in the station house. The train manager gave me a list of names of the people going on the tour and asked that I make sure that all 15 re-boarded the bus at every stop.

"Don't come back with only 14 people," the manager

said to me in a very stern, religious tone. "We won't be able to wait for one lost sheep."

He told everyone that the bus was leaving in five minutes and if anyone wanted to use the washrooms before boarding the bus, to do so right now. Lillian and I proceeded to the bus parked behind the station house. We spoke to the driver who was busy cleaning the mirrors on the bus. Boarding the bus we had a choice of seats. We sat down in the first seat behind the driver. About eight other travellers got on the bus and we waited for the others. A man and woman took the second seat across from us and I said hello to each person getting on the bus. I wanted to be able to recognize everyone, just in case I had to search for a lost passenger.

"When's the bus going to leave?" asked the man across the aisle after about five minutes of waiting.

"There are two more people to come," I replied. "There could be a lineup for the washrooms."

The final two boarded the bus, and I accounted for my 15 sightseers.

"Where the hell is the bus driver?" shouted the guy across the aisle. I leaned over to Lillian and whispered that I thought we might have a real live Archie Bunker with us on this bus.

"I paid money for a sightseeing trip and we're sitting here in the station's damn parking lot," roared Archie.

It was taking a bit of time, but the bus driver was wiping down the windows with a rubber strip on a long wooden handle. It had been raining and I noticed that the area around the station was quite muddy. This was a giant highway bus with luggage compartments under the seats. If we were going to tour Kalgoorlie, it would be best to have the windows as clean as possible. Also, it was in the evening and quite dark outside.

Bouncing up the steps and into the coach came the bus driver. With one big leap, she landed in the big swivel chair ahead of me. Only five feet tall and stretching one extra inch, the little ball of energy shouted out, "Are you ready to go?"

There was a loud "Yes!" from most everyone on the bus.

Now Archie of course, had his own remarks to say from across the aisle. In his rough, gruff, obnoxious voice, he piped up and said, "Where's the driver?"

With a smiling face and a pleasant small voice, the young woman sitting in the driver's seat replied, "I'm your driver."

Old Archie stood up and shaking his fist in the air said, "I'm not riding with a woman driver. Who do you think you are, getting on this big bus and telling us that you are going to drive this thing?"

He raved on, saying that if a woman was at the controls, then he was getting off the bus. I was just about to slide out of my seat so that I could be standing, as he was much bigger than me, and tell him to be quiet or to get off the bus, when that firecracker of a little woman turned on her booming voice so everyone in the coach could hear her.

"Listen mister," she said. "If you stay on this bus you are going to see some ore-moving vehicles that look like giant dump trucks at the gold mine tonight. Their wheels are as high as the roof on this bus. Now hear this, I used to drive one of those trucks five days a week at the mine. This bus is so small compared to those earthmovers that it seems like a toy to me."

Switching to a voice that sounded a little more on the mellow side, the young woman said, "I have two boys at home and I switched jobs so I could be home more regular hours with my kids."

She noted that the mine works 24 hours a day, every day of the year. When working there, she was on shift duty and often worked nights and weekends when her boys were home from school. She drove those monster trucks at the mine for six years.

"We Aussie women can handle anything," she said. And I certainly believed her.

Archie sat down. He never spoke another word the whole bus trip. Maybe he'd learned his lesson by the put-down of a powerful little woman named Martha who stood up against a big bully. I felt sorry for Archie's wife, as she quietly sat through all of this unnecessary commotion at the beginning of an interesting evening. I thought I saw a little grin on her face when boisterous Archie sat down next to her again. I think she was pleased with the way the dispute ended.

During the tour I asked the passengers to tell us the country they were from. Most were simply homegrown Australians. Lillian and I introduced ourselves as being from Canada. There was a couple from New Zealand and a man from Hong Kong. Archie didn't say a word but his wife quietly announced that they were Americans.

Martha took us to a lookout where we could see just about the entire mine in operation. This open pit gold mine was so big that you could bury a major city in it. In 1893, an Irishman by the name of Paddy Hannan discovered gold nearly 600 km northwest of Perth in Australia's outback. The area was soon flooded with prospectors looking for their fortunes. It's like a contagious fever that spreads to all parts of the body and all parts of the land once one person cries, "Gold!"

The Super Pit is managed by Kalgoorlie Consolidated Gold Mines (KCGM) and is owned 50 percent by Newmont Australia Pty Ld. and 50 percent by Barrick Australia Pacific. Canadians are quite familiar with the name Barrick. It was University of Toronto graduate Peter Munk who founded Barrick Gold Corporation. He holds the honour of being a Companion of the Order of Canada, a distinction that few Canadians receive. His gold mining interests cover many countries, with Australia, Tanzania, and both North and South America being the most significant areas. Barrick Gold

Corporation with its headquarters in Toronto, Canada, is the largest gold mining company in the world. Kalgoorlie's Super Pit produces nearly 400,000 ounces of gold each year.

And yes, we saw those monster dump trucks that Martha told us she'd driven while working at the mine. It would take one man standing on the shoulders of another man to reach the top of the wheels on some of those giant vehicles. We watched the trucks load up with ore at the bottom of the pit and slowly weave their way back and forth around the curves and up the steep sides of the cavern to the top level of the mine area.

As one looked down into this unbelievable man-made hole in the ground, it made me think of America's Grand Canyon in Arizona. The difference, of course, is that man dug the Aussie's hole while Mother Nature provided the 1,800 metre (6,000 feet) deep hole in the American southwest. The mine is only a third of the depth of the Grand Canyon, but its 512 metres (1,680 feet) hole in the ground makes Niagara Falls look like nothing more than a rapid in the Niagara River. The Canadian side of the Falls claims a drop of 57 metres while its neighbor, the American Falls has a drop of 59 metres. Niagara Falls can at least claim to have the most water by volume pass over the falls of any place in the world. Kalgoorlie is envious of all that water, as it is always in short supply in the outback.

Leaving the gold mine behind, but not the 15 people whom I'd been given the responsibility for, we travelled into the city of Kalgoorlie. It was mid-evening there and quite dark except for the street lights and lights adorning the buildings. Some of the main streets were quite wide and in some areas of the city, hotels and saloons outnumbered the people on the streets. Kalgoorlie has a population of about 30,000, not far off the mark of decades ago when prospectors were swarming into the area looking for gold. When things didn't pan out for many of these early pioneers, they pulled up stakes and left. However, with the big mining companies involved in digging for gold, people have gravitated back to the city to work in the mine or the businesses that have sprung up in the urban community.

Kalgoorlie has never outlived its reputation of a Wild West town. When fights started in the saloons, it was not unusual to have them end up out on the streets. Some of the famous old hotels that still operate today include the Broken Hill Hotel, Exchange Hotel, Kalgoorlie Grand Hotel, Hannans Hotel, Palace Hotel, Picadilly Hotel, York Hotel and the interesting Star and Garter.

In those early days with thousands of men converging on the town, women were in short supply. This opened the door for the very profitable business of operating brothels. And don't for a moment think they've been eliminated in this day and age.

We had to be back at the station before the train left or we would be spending several days in this old Australian Wild West town. I think some of the male passengers may have enjoyed that kind of side trip.

"Wow," shouted a man sitting further back in the bus. "Did you see that?"

He was pointing at a window on the driver's side of the bus. He was sitting next to the window and his wife was sitting beside him on the aisle.

"Look at that!" he exclaimed, tapping his finger on the window. "I think we died and went to heaven! Wow!"

In response, his wife sitting next to him said, "From now on, keep your eyes looking straight ahead in this bus. No more window gazing!"

Other passengers laughed. The "wow" could have been anyone's call on that bus. Most of the passengers witnessed an unexpected performance in front of one of the saloons as we passed by. One man shouted to the bus driver to stop and back up. Another suggested we go around the block so we could pass by again.

What happened? Well, Lillian and I, like several others on the bus, were eyewitnesses to what would be a very unusual event at home. Remember, we are in the Australian outback where survival comes first and everything else is tolerated. The bus was slowly creeping along the street. I can't remember whether it was Hay Street or Hannan Street, you'll have to forgive me for forgetting with all of the excitement around us. Lillian had her head close to the very large bus window and I was peering around her shoulder watching the hotels and saloons slink by. It reminded me of the backlot at Warner Bros. Studio in California. We saw only a few men going in and out of the swinging doors at a couple of bars. If you wanted to see lots of people, you'd have to come back when the mine shift is over and everyone pours out of work and into the town's streets. It would feel more like the Fourth of July.

The bus was moving very slowly, at a snail's pace, to give us time to view the old west saloon buildings that lined the street, when all of a sudden those swinging doors swung out on one of the buildings. Out came a very attractive blond woman. She could have been Marilyn Monroe's twin sister, if she had one. This gorgeous woman stepped out onto the porch, letting the doors swing back and forth until they stopped behind her. She waved to us on the bus. This was a very friendly gesture on her part. On that warm outback night, she was wearing (very) short white shorts and a deep, rich red sleeveless top.

She waved again and some of the bus passengers waved back. All of a sudden, without warning, she took hold of her red sweater and pulled it up from her waist, tucking it in under her chin. And now you understand the "wow" factor from the fellow at the back of the bus.

There she stood, tall and proud like the Statue of Liberty welcoming newcomers to the United States, wearing high heels with her long, bare legs running up to those short shorts, with nothing covering her ample breasts. The beautiful Australian woman stood, welcoming bus travellers to her place for drinks and entertainment. Unlike Lady Liberty, a great big friendly smile on her face and a bare chest was the Kalgoorlie visitor's welcome.

One Aussie guy chirped up, "Ya'know mate, there're bigger than the melons in my garden." His tongue fumbled around a few more Aussie expressions that an interpreter would be required to decipher for the rest of us.

All eyes were on the one-woman welcoming committee on Kalgoorlie's saloon row.

"Com'n for a while!" she shouted. "Com'n and have some fun."

It was like the call of the wild. Kalgoorlie hasn't changed in a hundred years. Some of the passengers on the bus were stunned. Some laughed. Others were speechless. Some were embarrassed. I guess it was the unexpected that turned some faces bright red on the bus.

The fellow on the bus who first pointed out the friendly lady in front of the saloon had totally disregarded his wife's command not to look. He was staring out the window with both eyes wide open. His wife was watching too. It took some of the passengers a few minutes to adjust to what they just heard and saw in the frontier town. We didn't have time to stop and that was probably a good thing, as it was still my promise to the train manager to return all 15 passengers safely back to him. I'm afraid if we accepted the saloon maiden's call, we would have had a few passengers jump ship (or in this case, bus) and I'd be in the doghouse with the manager for losing some semi-precious cargo.

When we arrived back at the railway station and got off the bus, most people gave some money to our driver

Martha for taking good care of us and showing us the Kalgoorlie sights. I think in some people's minds, the Super Pit became secondary to the tour of the saloon and hotel district downtown. The latter seemed to be the talk of the passengers all the way back to the train. I did notice that even Archie Bunker, our across-the-aisle neighbor, gave Martha a tip. Good for him.

The Indian Pacific was soon rolling out of the station at Kalgoorlie on our overnight ride to Perth. Lillian and I planned to spend a few days in Perth and while there, we'd visit the Port of Fremantle before flying north to Darwin.

Leaving the train, we said goodbye to the train manager, the engineer and his assistant. The engineer hoped his picture would appear in my newspaper story. Sorry, editors have the final say. Unfortunately, his photos didn't make it, but several others did in my full-page feature on riding the rails Down Under. It appeared in a Canadian daily newspaper.

Lillian and I have been on other trains in Australia on various trips to that unique continent. I can't forget riding the famous Ghan train from Darwin in Australia's Northern Territory, off the Timor Sea, to the city of Adelaide that is located in the state of South Australia on the Gulf of St. Vincent in the Indian Ocean.

Whoa, the previous paragraph needs some clarification. As old George Washington would say, "I can't tell a lie."

Our train ticket was from Darwin, but on the night before we were to leave the frontier town and its hot, humid weather, a cyclone hit the northern part of the country, washing out a couple hundred kilometres of rail line running south from the town. Oh my! I'm not fond of bus travel, but the only way to get south from Darwin to a town called Katherine, where the train was waiting, was by bus. The Darwin airport was closed due to the storm, so it was bus or bust. We took the bus through flooded roadways and caught the train in Katherine. Someday Lillian and I will go back to Darwin and ride the train from there to Katherine, just to complete the journey.

FLY WITH ME

"Howdy, Partner!" – Walter (top left) meets some new friends in an old mining town. Lillian (top right) outside the deserted Calico mine.

Below, an old steam engine travels through the mountains in Colorado. These towns prospered with the gold rush, but ghost towns are all that remains.

WALTER W. GOWING

Walter and Lillian (top) welcome you to Cook, Australia. Three people still live in the town.

Green fees at the all-sand golf club (bottom) are $2.00. Walter was upset to have forgotten his clubs.

PART FOUR

PAN AM GIRL

CHAPTER TWELVE

JUST JEAN

This delightful and exciting story of Jean (Barrett) Fayle is a true account of an adventurous young Canadian woman who travelled more miles in six years as a flight attendant with Pan American Airlines than most people travel in a lifetime. It was an airline that I always wanted to fly on but unfortunately for me, it ceased operating before I had a chance. Pan Am began its humble 64 years in the air in 1927 and made its last flight in 1991.

Jean is a member of the Cambridge, Ontario branch of the Canadian Federation of University Women. She is also a member of Trinity Anglican Church in Cambridge (formerly Galt) which is coincidentally, the same church in which my parents were married in 1930, the year Jean was born.

I met Jean through her association with my wife Lillian, who is also a member of CFUW. I knew from the very first time I met Jean that there was a great story to be told. Always courteous and pleasant, she made conversation a relaxing event. Although I've interviewed thousands of people for my newspaper column over more than six decades, Jean was a challenge. Her speed with words and changing lanes from one subject to the next was sometimes outpacing my lead pencil. I still like to take notes with pencil and paper. Her experiences flying with Pan Am could fill a book. She's earned her keep in this one.

Jean was born on January 12, 1930 in Niagara Falls, Ontario. Her father was Thomas W.C. Barrett from England and her mother, Alta May Williams, was a Niagara Falls local. As a young woman, Jean's mother worked as a bank clerk for the Imperial Bank of Canada in St. Catharines when she married the dashing young Englishman. He always wanted to be a farmer and so they moved to the Grand Valley area in Ontario where he operated a small mixed farming operation. Jean was the oldest of five girls in the family, and her mother died when Jean was just 11 years old.

As a young girl, Jean and her sisters walked two miles to a one-room schoolhouse that had grades stretching from one to eight. In the centre of the room sat a potbelly stove that kept the school cozy during the cold and blustery winters. The students' teacher was just an 18-year old girl herself.

In 1941, Jean's father moved the family to Galt, Ontario. During the Second World War, her father worked for the Art Metal Industries, a company that made airplane parts for planes used by the Royal Canadian Air Force.

Graduating from Galt Collegiate Institute in 1948, Jean went into training at the Toronto East General Hospital and finished her studies as a nurse in 1951. She spent the next year working at the hospital. Canadian nurses were in demand in the United States, and so it was off to St. Barnabas Hospital in Minneapolis, Minnesota for Jean for the next year. The northern state that borders Ontario and Manitoba made Jean feel right at home. "They liked Canadians and treated us well," she said.

In 1954, seeking excitement and adventure, Jean accepted a nursing position at a small 250-bed hospital at Great Neck, Long Island. While working on Long Island, she realized that she was on New York City's doorstep, the headquarters of Pan American Airlines. It was one of the first airlines to have routes around the world.

Becoming a flight attendant with Pan Am was harder to do than getting into the White House on Capitol Hill, or breaking into the Bank of England. The airline recruited their beautiful young women from all over the world. Education and language skills were important, but applicants had to meet physical measurement requirements as well. Pan Am was noted for having the most beautiful hostesses on board their planes of any airline in existence. The airline hired girls from England, France, and of course from all 50 states in the Union. It was a matter of "who you knew" that got you an interview and a job. It just so happened that Jean knew someone who knew a member on the airline's board of directors. Jean was called for an interview, passed all of the tests, and being a registered nurse helped her cause immensely. In those days, Pan Am carried one nurse on each flight. Jean was happy to put on the classy uniform that the girls wore working as stewardesses on Pan Am. Each girl flying through the fluffy white clouds across the blue skies was every bit as gorgeous as the highest paid models on a Paris runway, or the fabulous movie stars who captured audiences from the Hollywood screens.

Most of Jean's flights were lengthy long-haul trips out of New York City across the Atlantic Ocean to countries in Africa, Asia and Europe, including the countries around the Mediterranean.

Jean bravely flew to some of the most dangerous, exotic cities that even today present red flags to North American travellers. And what better way to reach these destinations during the 1950s and 60s than to fly and get paid for doing it? Despite her busy schedule flying back and forth across the Atlantic, Jean found time to enroll in Columbia University's nursing program and graduated from the private New York school with a BSc (N.Ed) in 1959.

As a flight attendant, Jean had the opportunity to cross paths with world leaders who were globe trotting to their next destination. She got to know them personally as they flew on private charter flights using Pan Am or on some of the airline's regularly scheduled overseas flights.

How about flying with the General Secretary of the United Nations and his staff? Jean was on a flight from New York City to London, England in 1958, as part of the crew who looked after Dag Hammarskjold and his staff. He was the second person (and the youngest ever) to serve as head of the UN, following Secretary-General Trygve Lie, who was from Norway and held the office from February 1946 to November 1952. Hammarskjold held the office from April 1953 until his death in September 1961. Hammarskjold was born in Sweden and became the youngest chairman of the Bank of Sweden. Prior to assuming the UN's top spot, he was deputy foreign minister of Sweden. Jean recalled his politeness and courteous manner toward the flight attendants. Jean likes to remember the good flights, as some passengers on flights were extremely obnoxious. Dag Hammarskjold was one of the good guys.

The outstanding statesman was killed in a DC6 airplane crash in 1961 en route to Africa's Congo to negotiate a cease-fire after learning about fighting between non-combatant UN forces and Katangese troops. There was very little left of the propeller-driven plane that crashed in Northern Rhodesia, now Zambia. An investigation by the UN failed to find the cause of the mysterious crash. There have always been questions unanswered concerning the players involved in Hammarskjold's death. Who would gain by killing the Secretary-General of the United Nations?

The participants involved with great interest in his trip to Ndola in the Congo, were the Soviet Union that was backing the Congolese government; Moise Tshombe, leader of the breakaway mineral-rich province of Katanga; the former colonial power of Belgium; numerous Western mining interests; and the Republic of Congo.

Jean felt a genuine mournfulness at Hammarskjold's tragic death. Her first flight as a stewardess with Pan Am was aboard a Douglas DC6 in 1955, the same type of aircraft that crashed in Africa, killing Hammarskjold and 15 others. The statesman received the Nobel Prize posthumously.

A tall, lanky man often boarded flights that Jean was working for the long haul across the Atlantic. The irony in this man travelling by Pan Am passenger aircraft could only be realized if you knew that he was the first pilot to fly solo nonstop across the Atlantic. On May 20, 1927, Charles Lindbergh took off from Roosevelt Field, near New York City, at 7:52 a.m., headed for Paris, France. He reached his destination, Le Bourget Field, on May 21 at 10:21 p.m. local time. He had flown 3,600 miles (5,790 kilometres) in 33 ½ hours.

Lindbergh became instantly famous, a household name in homes on both sides of the Atlantic. When he arrived back in New York, the city went wild. Hundreds of thousands of citizens filled the streets to welcome Lindbergh like a Roman soldier bringing the spoils back to the emperor. At City Hall, Mayor Walker said, "New York City is yours. I don't give it to you, you won it."

The newspapers had a field day with Lindbergh's story, calling him "Lucky Lindy" and crowning him the world's greatest aviator. He was the number one news item in every city that he visited.

It was years later when he boarded Jean's Pan Am flights to cross the Atlantic. He wasn't the same effervescent young flyer who had taken the aviation world by storm. He was a quiet, reserved passenger who didn't interact with any of the other passengers and spoke very few words with the crew.

"Don't tell anyone I'm on this plane," he said to Jean as he headed to a seat at the rear of the aircraft. He wanted to be by himself, alone and quiet. Lindbergh was an advisor to the Pan American board of directors.

Following his famous flight and all the publicity it attracted, another news-breaking story hit the media. Charles and his wife Anne Spencer Morrow had suffered a tragic disaster when their first child, 20-month-old Charles Jr. was kidnapped from their home in New Jersey in 1932. The shock was devastating and even worse news soon followed.

A ransom of $70,000 (approximately $1.2 million in 2016) was paid to meet the demand of the kidnapper, but the little boy was never returned. Just less than three months later, the dead boy's body was found. Bruno Hauptmann, a carpenter, was arrested and charged with the little boy's murder. He was convicted and executed in 1936.

Charles Lindbergh asked for no special treatment when flying with Pan Am. He would ride to the aircraft on the crew's bus and requested no special attention. He just wanted to be by himself, sitting at the back.

Wining and dining with the world's top lawmakers and politicians became almost a routine for young Jean. A chartered flight to Germany from New York in the fall of 1960 was a remarkable experience that Jean encountered while getting to know the right people. It was a 'Crusade for Freedom' flight.

This flight of American dignitaries was to celebrate the 10th anniversary of the United States presentation of the Freedom Bell (called the Freiheitglocke in German) as a symbol of the new Germany and its stand against communism in East Germany and other parts of Europe.

Supreme U.S. Commander General Dwight D. Eisenhower was one of the founders of the Crusade for Freedom that resulted in the American people presenting West Berlin with the Freedom Bell in the fall of 1950. Assisting Eisenhower was General Lucius Clay, known for supervising the airlift to save the people of West Berlin, an area surrounded by Russian communists. Clay was given the title of "Father of the Berlin Airlift" for his efforts to push against the communist aggression that threatened the day.

The magnificent 10-ton Freedom Bell was made in England and first shipped to New York for a ticker tape parade before visiting 21 U.S. cities. The bell gathered 16 million American signatures before being shipped to hang in the West Berlin city hall. Inscribed on the bell are these words: "That this world under God shall have a new birth of freedom." The mayor of West Berlin at the time was Ernst Reuter and he pledged that Germany "will never rest or relax until freedom will shine over the countries of Eastern Europe that are at present forced to live in slavery."

Ten years later, on board Jean's plane winging its way across the Atlantic with Washington politicians and members of the judiciary, was one particularly well-known United States District Court Judge for the District of Columbia. Luther W. Youngdahl was an exuberant and happy sort of fellow who Jean enjoyed long conversations with. The judge's record for outstanding service to his country included three terms as a Republican Governor of Minnesota.

At his death in June of 1978, the Minneapolis Star Tribune had this to say about Judge Youngdahl: "As a lawyer, judge, Minnesota governor and spokesman for Christianity, Youngdahl left his mark on Minnesota and the nation for six decades."

The newspaper highlighted one of Judge Youngdahl's most famous cases from 1952 at the height of the anti-Communist campaign of Sen. Joseph McCarthy. The Star Tribune said, "…the judge dismissed as unconstitutional, key parts of the government's case against Owen J. Lattimore, a prime target of the McCarthy campaign." Citizen-bashing McCarthy testified that Lattimore, a professor at Johns Hopkins University was "the top Soviet espionage agent in the United States."

In dismissing the indictment against Lattimore, Judge Youngdahl wrote in defense of the First Amendment: "When public excitement runs high as to the alien ideologies, is the time when we must be particularly alert to not impair the ancient landmarks set up in the Bill of Rights."

The judge was sometimes known as "the governor

who's against sin" for his many crusades against such things as slot machines.

Judge Youngdahl impressed Jean as he went up and down the aisle on the plane repeating a poem to every single passenger. Jean requested a copy of the poem, receiving it in the mail in a personalized letter from the judge.

United States District Court
For the District of Columbia
Washington 1, D.C.

Luther W. Youngdahl
United States District Judge

November 2, 1960

Dear Jean:

First let me say how much we all appreciated the wonderful service we had from you, Toni and the other members of the crew on our Crusade for Freedom trip Europe. It was a memorable trip.

I am enclosing the poem you requested. I hope the future will hold good health and happiness for you.

*Sincerely yours,
(signed) Luther Youngdahl*

Miss Jean C. Barrett
440 Riverside Drive
Apartment 101
New York 27, N.Y.

THE LITTLE CHAP WHO FOLLOWS ME

A careful man I want to be
A little fellow follows me
I do not dare to go astray
  For fear he'll go the self-same way.
I cannot once escape his eyes,
  What'er he sees me do he tries
Like me he says he is going to be
  That little chap who follows me.
He thinks that I am good and fine
Believes in every word of mine
The base in me he must not see,
  That little chap who follows me.
I must remember as I go
  Thru summer's sun and winter's snow
I am building for the years to be
  That little chap who follows me.

There was a lot more for Jean than just catering to the passengers on that chartered plane to Berlin. Once there, in Germany's capital city, the airline crew was taken with the passengers to all of the champagne receptions and official events involving both the U.S. government diplomats and the officials from the German government.

At Berlin's City Hall, the world-famous Willy Brandt, Mayor of Berlin welcomed everyone including the Pan Am flight crew.

"It was a thrill to receive a miniature Freedom Bell from Willy," Jean said. "I was so lucky to be involved in such great functions and meet so many world leaders." Brandt was mayor of Berlin from 1957 to 1966. In 1969 he became Chancellor of the Federal Republic of Germany. In 1970, Time Magazine named him "Man of the Year."

"I had the privilege of meeting Mrs. Brandt," said Jean. "Who insisted I call her by her first name, Rut. She was a delightful person and we chatted for quite some time."

Rut was formerly Rut Hansen of Norway. She was Willy's second wife and had three sons while married to him for 32 years. They divorced in 1980. Willy's first wife for seven years was another Norwegian named Anna Thorkildsen. They had one daughter before splitting. Willy married his third wife in 1983, the former Brigitte Seebacher. Willy was 70 years old at the time and Brigitte was 37.

There was another marriage of a kind that Willy was involved in for four months in late 1936. After fleeing Germany to Norway in 1933 to avoid the political-military machine of the Nazis, Willy (whose real name was Herbert Ernest Karl Frahm) adopted his name, Willy Brandt. He was a left-wing socialist whose ideas were opposite to the growing Nazi party led by Adolf Hitler.

In 1936 he returned to Germany as a student under the name of Gunnar Gaasland. Willy, now Gunnar, married Gertrud Meyer in a mock wedding to save her from persecution or deportation by the Nazis. Meyer and Brandt had been "associates" in Norway for the past three years.

In 1937, during the Spanish Civil War, Willy worked as a journalist and was always just one step ahead of the authorities. In 1940 he was arrested in Norway by the German occupying forces but managed to escape to Sweden. After the Second World War, Willy went back to Germany and began a new life and a new career as a socialist politician. He rose to become the mayor of West Berlin, Chancellor of the Republic of Germany and received the Nobel Peace Prize.

"What a remarkable man," Jean said. "I'm so proud to have met him."

WALTER W. GOWING

CHAPTER THIRTEEN

"SIERRA PAPPA!"

Early in the morning on Wednesday, October 7, 2009, Lillian and I went down the gangway from a small ship docked in the Port of Tema. The sky was cloudy but soon cleared, revealing a bright sun. The temperature was hot, but not humid. We were only about five degrees north of the equator. Tema is Ghana's main port and the sea entrance to the country's capital city of Accra. About one million people live in the metropolitan area of Accra. We were to have a police escort for the one-hour drive into Accra but the police failed to show up at the dock. We ventured on into the capital on our own. We were glad to be there because of friends of ours, Dr. Daniel and Afua Ayim, back in Cambridge. They were originally natives of Ghana. Dan is a retired veterinarian and a past governor of a Lions Club district.

We were on our way from Dover, England to Cape Town, South Africa when we made our stop in Ghana. It's important to note several other stops on our long journey south from England.

We stopped in at Dakar, Senegal, the most westerly point of land in Africa. As you look at the continent of Africa, picture that big bulge that sticks out into the Atlantic Ocean in the northwest region. Lillian had been warned to make sure that she was well-dressed with long clothes and especially to have her shoulders covered. Senegal is a strict Muslim country. It was not even proper for me to wear shorts. Our guide, Mam, explained one of the differences between Shiite Muslims and Sunni Muslims.

He explained that Shiites are allowed to marry for one day and divorce the next day. This amounts to a one-night stand. Sunnis believe in a more traditional marriage, according to Mam.

Our next port of call was Senegal's neighbouring country of Gambia. This independent country has a population of about two million. Our small ship had an advantage that bigger ships lacked – the capability to sail up rivers away from the ocean. Gambia's capital city of Banjul is located on St. Mary's Island at the mouth of the Gambia River. We cruised up the river for about 22 miles before docking and explored the nearby land and villages. On our way downstream we visited Banjul where Lillian did some batik painting on a cloth at an outdoor factory. I purchased a magnificent 26-inch wooden carving of a hunter carrying the game he captured.

We left the Port of Banjul late in the afternoon with the idea of cruising south, just off the African coast, to our next destination – Ghana. The captain planned to follow the coastline past Guinea, Sierra Leone, Liberia and Cote d'Ivoire to reach Port Tema in Ghana. This is a most interesting area of West Africa. Since the early days of European traders to this part of the dark continent, various countries along the coastline were given names relating to the main products they traded.

The present day country of Liberia was known as the Grain Coast for its spices called "grains of paradise" once profusely traded by the Africans to the Portuguese. Cote d'Ivoire's trading name of Ivory Coast reflected the ivory trade engaged with foreigners. Hundreds of elephants were slaughtered for their ivory tusks. Modern day Ghana was once known as the Gold Coast due to its export of gold. It also shared in the export of slaves. Many slaves were brought from neighbouring countries and sold to English, Dutch and Danish traders. The Slave Coast name was reserved for the countries of Togo and Benin. This area was one of Africa's most densely populated areas and the slave population fed the Atlantic slave trade for more than 300 years. It is estimated that about three million slaves were exported across the Atlantic to the New World.

Early in the evening, after sailing from Banjul, the sun had yet to set. The captain received a radio message that changed everything for us. The messaged signaled danger ahead. Pirates were operating along the coastline just south of our location. Captain William Kent, master of the ship, decided to change course and head out further into the Atlantic. He would make a big loop before returning near the shoreline south of Ghana. He notified all passengers and crew via the intercom about the change in plans and followed up with printed instructions delivered to everyone's stateroom.

If pirates are sighted, the words "Sierra Pappa" will be announced over the public address system. We should immediately clear the decks and retreat to our cabins. Further orders said to close our drapes, stay away from the windows and lie on the floor with the lights out. I immediately got my cameras ready and prepared my method of taking pictures of the pirates, if and when they attacked. After all, I am a journalist and I wasn't going to miss this story for anything. The captain warned us that he might have to manoeuver the ship at high speeds with some erratic turns, if necessary, to escape the pirates. It was a night of suspense.

The next morning we sailed into the Port of Tema without encountering the pirates. Battling pirates off the coast of Africa in the high seas of the Atlantic would have been a great story. "If you'd lived to tell about it," Lillian reminded me.

Ghana is a most interesting country to visit. Their National Museum is considered to be one of the finest sub-Saharan museums in Africa. It has some of the greatest resources on the slave trade anywhere in the world. We enjoyed the Palm Hotel, where Lillian found her five darling, highly polished, little wood-carved snails. I now see them every day at home, as they sit on a side table in our living room, near the fireplace.

We had an impressive visit to the Nkrumah Mausoleum, a memorial in honour of Dr. Kwame Nkrumah, the first president of Ghana. He's the man who brings us back to our Pan Am girl, Jean Fayle.

Jean was assigned to a chartered Pan Am flight from New York to Accra, Ghana in 1960. It stopped in Lisbon, Portugal to refuel before flying on to its final destination in Africa. Jean was quite used to this type of flight and thought nothing of it until she saw the passenger list. Among the dozen and a half names, most of them she couldn't pronounce, was one that stood out.

Dr. Kwame Nkrumah had become the first President of Ghana when the British relinquished control of the country in 1957. He and his entourage were in New York to visit the United Nations and Jean would help to see they had a good flight home. Now, three years later, the country was a republic with a president and a one-party system. It is a member of the Commonwealth of Nations, as is Canada. Today, it is a multi-party state after a number of coups and unsettled political situations.

In the air, out over the Atlantic Ocean and nearing the European coast, Jean and some members of her crew were up and ready for a day of work. It was still early in the morning after their long flight over the briny sea, but time to get things moving aboard the plane. Some of the passengers were up and moving about. Jean and her crewmates prepared breakfast and attempted to serve the passengers who were awake.

"No breakfast," said a passenger. "Not now."

All of the other passengers who were awake said the same thing.

"Are you not hungry?" asked Jean.

"Oh yes," replied one young man. "But we cannot eat

before the President."

Jean and her crew witnessed many anomalies during their Pan Am flights, but this was the first time for an eating protocol.

It was only recently, in a conversation with Dr. Ayim, that he told me about the tradition of who eats first in Ghana. Historically, the oldest man is served first at mealtime. Also, he selects whom he wishes to eat with. This is respect for the elderly and also for someone in a high-ranking position, like the president. Not eating before the president may have seemed strange to the North American flight crew, but for the Ghanaians on board, it was perfectly natural to wait.

Finally, arriving in Accra, the president was the first to deplane. He stood at the top of the steps, waved to a small crowd below on the tarmac and slowly alighted step by step. In moments he was gone in a shiny black limousine. He left a message for the crew, thanking them for the kind hospitality and requesting that they accept his invitation to visit his home the following day and enjoy a reception in their honour.

The next day, Jean and her crew were dressed in the very best and chauffeured to the Republic of Ghana's Golden Jubilee House, the official residence and presidential palace of the president. This was like a dream, a fairytale, especially for the female members of the Pan Am crew. It was like attending Cinderella's Ball.

President Osagyefo Dr. Kwame Nkrumba welcomed his visitors to the reception at his magnificent home. He took time to speak to each of his guests personally. He was a delightful host.

Jean was flabbergasted with the occasion. It was almost overwhelming for a girl who attended a one-room school in rural Ontario to be in these surroundings with the head of an African nation. It was an Alice in Wonderland moment in her life.

Usually flights to Africa meant a four or five day layover for the crew. They had to wait for the next Pan Am plane to arrive so that they could relieve the flying crew and take the plane on to its next destination or back to New York. On some occasions, Jean and her crew would leave Ghana on a flight to Johannesburg, the largest city in South Africa.

As you may recall, Lillian and I have been to South Africa numerous times because Cape Town is my favourite city in the world. One early November morning in 2003, Lillian and I headed for the Johannesburg airport for a flight to Victoria Falls. A couple of days earlier we were in South Africa's administrative capital city, Pretoria, only 50 kilometres north of Johannesburg. In Pretoria, Jacaranda trees line the streets, a display of the most brilliant colours you'll see anywhere in the world. From Johannesburg, we flew to Zimbabwe to see the falls. We stayed at the palatial Victoria Falls Hotel. This hotel was originally built by the British in 1904 to serve as accommodation for the workers of the Cape-to-Cairo railway. The hotel played host for several royal visits over the years, including King George VI and his family (including then-Princess

Elizabeth, now Queen Elizabeth II) in 1947. During this royal tour, the young Elizabeth celebrated her 21st birthday on April 21, and gave a radio message recorded in Cape Town.

"I declare before you all that my whole life whether it be long or short shall be devoted to your service and the service of our great imperial family to which we all belong," the Princess said in her speech, mentioning the great privilege of belonging to the world-wide commonwealth.

She certainly lived up to her promise, celebrating her 90th birthday in 2016. Up to that point, she'd visited 51 of the 53 current Commonwealth member nations.

It always amazed me how royalty traveled to these remote places before the jet era.

Sitting in the hotel's luxurious Grand State Room adorned with original oil paintings of distinguished royalty stretching from floor to ceiling, one felt just like a member of the Royal Family. If you attempted to wipe the sweat from your forehead, before you could move, a houseboy was right there mopping your brow with a cool wet cloth. If your drinking glass dropped from full to half full, someone refilled it immediately with whatever you were drinking. (I must report that they had excellent lemonade, although most drinks were much stronger.)

If you are concerned about what you are about to eat, always ask about the food, especially at a buffet. One evening in the lavish hotel dining room, the buffet contained very large snake steaks, crocodile tail, lizard and various other local animal parts and insects. It was the finest food if you were used to this kind of diet.

I paid cash, Zimbabwe dollars, one night for dinner. I couldn't bring home a suitcase full of money. I paid $120,000 cash for Lillian and I to eat dinner at the hotel on our last evening at Victoria Falls. It was a stack of paper money about a foot tall. Really, only about $45 in Canadian currency. The tip was extra, in American dollars. You can see the advantages that North Americans have in travelling to many less-fortunate nations. Visiting there does help the local economy and provides jobs for the native people.

Victoria Falls is one of the world's greatest falls, stretching 1.6 kilometres in length and dropping 108 metres. By comparison, Niagara Falls back home drops only 51 metres, less than half of the mighty Victoria. The falls was named after Queen Victoria of England by David Livingston, the first European to discover the falls in 1855. About a stone's throw from the falls is a statue of Livingston. Lillian took my picture with Mr. Livingston's statue, standing with his left hand on his hip, feet set wide apart. I posed just like him for the photo, but Livingston beat me to the falls by some 148 years.

Now, our friend and Pan Am stewardess Jean Fayle saw Victoria Falls on flights from Accra, Ghana to Johannesburg, South Africa. We are one up on Jean in this location because we have both flown over the falls and traversed the surrounding area on foot. Of course,

Jean's story is still quite unique.

As Jean recalls, the pilots in her days with Pan Am were certainly more adventurous than the men and women in the cockpit today. They didn't have all the high-tech computer gadgets that clutter up the dashboards of aircraft nowadays. The pilots really flew the planes in those earlier days, hands on. If pilots wanted to stray a little off the charted flight plan to show the passengers something special, they did. And Victoria Falls was indeed very special.

When Jean's plane approached the falls, the pilot announced that passengers should remain in their seats because they'd be making several circles over the falls, tilting the plane's wings one way and then the other so passengers on both sides of the aisle would get an equal view of the water cascading over the falls.

The plane dropped from 16,000 feet, down, down, almost out of the sky. It leveled off at 500 feet above the roaring water below. Sometimes circling the many channels of the Zambezi River that was sending its sparkling water crashing over the precipice of what appeared to be the end of the earth. What a fantastic sight. Passengers got a look at rhinos in the middle of the river, just upstream from the falls. Look out, there are crocodiles nestling along the shoreline. As the plane took to higher altitudes, it sometimes just cleared the tree line on the Zambia side of the river, the fourth longest river in Africa after the more widely-known Nile, Congo and Niger rivers.

On one of our trips, two former Cambridge

schoolteachers (you may recall Murray Jull and Larry Rawlings from ostrich racing earlier in this book) shared a small boat with us not far above the falls. At times it was scary, but we made it across from Zimbabwe to Zambia and back again without the rhinos and crocodiles getting us or plummeting our small vessel over one of the biggest river drops on this globe.

Lillian and I agree with Jean, it truly is one of the most fantastic and breathtaking sights in the world.

WALTER W. GOWING

CHAPTER FOURTEEN

OOPS, SORRY MR. KENNEDY!

Scoop!

This story has never been told before. Pan American Airlines didn't want it told. Beyond the crew of this chartered flight by the Democratic Party of the United States of America, no one really knew of the incident that took place thousands of feet in the air.

This story takes place on a Super-6 Clipper winging its way across the United States, as told by the young Canadian nurse, flight attendant and adventurer Jean Fayle.

As I approached the handsome, relaxed-looking man who would become the next president of the United States of America, he looked up and smiled. His jacket had been discarded and his tie was missing from around his neck. The pale blue shirt looked like it had been freshly starched. He always appeared to be impeccably dressed, even when relaxing or working on a speech in the election race for the highest office in the country. One could even say the most powerful office in the world.

It was 1960 and young Senator John F. Kennedy

was running for president. His opponent, Richard M. Nixon had what some political pundits thought was a running leg-up advantage. Nixon had been the vice-president to a very popular Dwight D. Eisenhower. Before becoming president, General Eisenhower led the Allied forces in Europe during the Second World War.

As a Pan American Airlines stewardess, I had one of the classiest jobs in the world. I had the world at my feet. When you are 20,000 feet up in the air, where else could the world be?

The American Queen, the mighty Statue of Liberty, was planted on the doorstep of New York City on October 28, 1886. As you left New York, she was like an angel giving her blessing on your trip, whether it be by ship or plane. The inspiration for Lady Liberty came from a Frenchman, Edouard Laboulaye, a politician and historian. He greatly admired the freedom and liberty of the American people. His friend and sculptor, Frederic Auguste Bartholdi made the majestic lady in France. He initially intended for her to guard the Suez Canal with her torch. Instead, this woman with the face of his mother ended up off Bedloe's Island in Upper New York Bay. Today, Egypt has its great pyramids, the United States has the Statue of Liberty, and Pan Am Airways had the most attractive stewardesses in the skies.

"Mr. Kennedy," I said, as I shyly approached him. He was mulling over one of his speeches he would

give at another political rally. There were several stops for us on this chartered trip. We were flying across the continent from New York to San Francisco. Along with the candidate were several top aides and a few members of the media on board.

He was so gentlemanly, so congenial, so precise, so charming, so... and on and on. He was it!

I had both hands on the little silver tray as I walked down the aisle of the plane, dressed in my sleek-blue uniform. On my little tray was a cup and saucer filled with tea. Nice, hot, relaxing tea. Just what a man running for the president's office needed to unwind amidst a busy, hectic schedule. If he wins this race, he gets the keys to the White House and he can sit back and put his feet up on that big desk in the Oval Office.

"Mr. Kennedy," I repeated. "I brought you a cup of tea."

Holding the tray with my left hand, I picked up the small china saucer holding the floral-detailed cup with my right hand. Some steam was evaporating from the cup. The tea was extremely hot.

The handsome Mr. Kennedy smiled at me and with his New England accent said, "Thank you very much."

I leaned over just a bit as I reached out with the hot

cup of tea.

WHAM.

What just happened?

The floor of the aircraft had dropped about a foot, maybe more. Instantly the plane had dropped, as if the bottom had fallen out. We had flown into a small air pocket. No warning, just hang on to your seat and hope that your seatbelt is fastened. That kind of advice wasn't going to help me standing there, holding a serving tray in one hand and a scalding hot cup of tea in the other.

Picture this in slow motion: the plane flies into a void in the air and instantly drops several feet. Everyone fastened in his or her seat drops with it. It's a bit of a jolt, but no damage is done. If you aren't used to flying, it's a bit of a frightening moment.

Now, I dropped with the plane. My feet never left the floor. My left hand never released the polished tray. Down it went with me. My right hand had a firm grip on the saucer and the cup nestled inside of the ring of the saucer. Both dropped with me as the plane took the quick plunge downward. Gosh, for a fleeting fraction of a second in time, everything appeared to be copacetic on the plane, save for a little (and literal) bump.

But what's floating in the air? Me, the tray, the cup

and the saucer all dropped together, but the tea, that's another thing. It didn't have its seatbelt fastened. There it was, suspended in midair. It was liquid English Breakfast – hot, steaming and hanging there.

Time had stopped. What I was seeing was all taking place in the blink of an eye. There it was, hot, hot tea floating in the air right in front of John F. Kennedy.

At that moment, with the tea floating between a passenger and me, the flight attendant, how could anyone even recall his own name? That tea just hung, suspended in the air, all by itself.

There was surely going to be a collision when Kennedy's body moved forward and made contact with the suspended hot tea.

And then it did.

The tea splashed all down the front of his freshly-pressed shirt. The painful grimace on his face instantly reflected the agony that Kennedy felt from the collision of body and tea. The sign of the pain inflicted by the scalding tea penetrating his cotton shirt and flooding over the skin of his chest was summed up in a guttural sound that came from his throat.

"Ahhhhh!" groaned Kennedy, as he felt the liquid

stinging his chest through the shirt.

"I'm sorry Mr. Kennedy!" I said, the words filled with compassion.

"It's not your fault," he quickly replied.

"This flight is like my PT boat," the scalded main said, wincing. During the Second World War, Kennedy was the skipper of a U.S. Navy PT boat. Assigned to duty off the Solomon Islands in the South Pacific, he was involved in some real war action. In the darkness of night on August 2, 1943, his little PT boat was cut in half by a much larger Japanese destroyer. Two of his crew were instantly killed. The remaining 10 swam to shore at daybreak after a night of clinging to the severely damaged boat. Kennedy injured his back during the disaster.

During the election campaign, Kennedy's handlers didn't want any reference made to his injured back. War wounds may sound patriotic, but some voters want to elect only a healthy president. During this tempest in a teapot, I realized that Kennedy was wearing a back brace. Following the election for president and after moving into the White House, it was impossible to keep the back brace a secret from the public.

The bumpy ride in the air probably had reminded the former naval officer of waves hitting the front of his vessel on a rough night in the Pacific Ocean. The sudden shock of the hot tea hitting his chest like *the body shock he received when his boat was rammed by the Japanese destroyer in the darkness of night. Unexpected and very painful.*

As the tea attacked his skin, the plane leveled out and the flight was back on course. The passenger, not so much back to normal.

My nurse's training kicked in without hesitation. I reached for the front of his shirt and said, "Let me check out your chest for burns."

"I will be alright," yelped Kennedy as he tightened his face, revealing the excruciating pain of the burn I'd surely find below.

One by one the buttons gave way to an open shirt and a hairy chest wrenching in pain.

"Someone bring me the first aid kit immediately!" I ordered like a field commander on the battlefield. There was a jar of cream in the kit and I quickly unscrewed the top and with two fingers, scooped out a glob of white putty. Swish and onto the chest of Kennedy went the cream. Delicately swirling it around with my fingers, I knew I was working against time. I didn't want the air to get at the burn before I had a chance to cover it. Any trace of fear or confusion disappeared from my mind. It was business as usual for this nurse. It didn't matter whether or not I was thousands of feet in the air, on a bobbing ship in the ocean, or even with a desert

caravan, I was a very capable nurse doing my job.

A few minutes later, an ungrateful head steward had some uncomplimentary things to say to me.

"This will have to be recorded," the over-efficient flight boss said. "Watch what you do in the future."

I was embarrassed enough without some unpleasant member of the crew threatening me. For a few moments, I wondered if I would lose my job, even if it wasn't really my fault.

It was a long chartered flight, stopping at a few cities across the vast span of America. The crew was busy looking after the needs of the passengers and the passengers were busy with their own politics.

At the end of the flight, Mr. Kennedy shook hands with each member of the crew. If anyone was noticing, he squeezed my hand just a little bit longer and a little bit harder than that of the others. In his boyish Boston accent, he said, "Thank you Jean for all your kindness."

The genuine words from someone who was about to become the 35th President of the United States were so greatly appreciated.

CHAPTER FIFTEEN

THE OPIUM DEN

The experiences of Jean Fayle would make a great movie or television series. She's visited everywhere from gold mines in South Africa to an opium den in Thailand. Maybe the opium den episode should be explained.

Opium comes from a plant and is the source of many medicines including morphine, codeine and heroin. These drugs are under strict governmental and medical control and are used in cases of severe pain. Opium is made from the juice of the opium variety of poppy flower. However, some people use opium as an escape from reality. It is highly addictive. Addicts sniff, eat, smoke or are injected with opium. It can carry the user into a stupefying world that ranges from soothing to violent unpleasantness.

What's a girl like Jean doing in a place like hell's hole of opium dealers and users? The answer to that started way back on a Pan Am flight into Bangkok, Thailand. She was serving a male passenger his meals and drinks on the flight, and they'd exchanged pleasant conversation. In the lobby of the crew's hotel in Bangkok, Jean ran into the same passenger and they chatted again. He mentioned he wanted to visit an opium den. It was a mystery to him and he thought it would be a very interesting story to tell his friends back home in the United States.

Jean agreed – it would be an extremely interesting story to tell.

Today when she recalls the tale, Jean exclaims, "I was sometimes very foolish but I was young and adventurous."

Bangkok is Thailand's capital city with about six million people. I can attest to the beauty of the many golden-domed Buddhist temples. Thai puppet shows and classical dancers always intrigued Lillian and me when visiting the vibrant city in Southeast Asia. The streets are generally crowded and narrow with more old buildings than new ones. Living standards are far below that of North America. There are areas in the city that at night a body guard is a prudent idea.

Jean and her newly acquainted friend threw all caution to the wind and asked the hotel doorman to get them a taxi. Like cabs in most cities, the drivers don't get out of the car, you just open the back door and climb right in. Now, if this is a three-wheel tutu, you just slide in behind the driver's narrow bench seat and have an open-air ride to your destination. This time it was a yellow and red automobile. It was an old one, with a few dents on the fenders and doors.

"Take us to an opium den," commanded the two passengers.
The driver had already moved the cab a few feet when the request was made. He stopped the car, turned his

head around and said something to Jean and her friend in Thai. He repeated himself in English.

"Opium den? Opium den?" he said.

"That's right, take us to an opium den," said the male passenger. "A good one."

Is there a difference between good opium dens and bad ones?

"Sure," repeated Jean. "We want to see what an opium den is really like."

The cab driver turned back, looking at the two passengers one more time and said, "You sure? You want opium den?"

"Yes, opium den," they said in unison back to him.

After about a 30-minute trip of zigzagging around other automobiles (mostly taxis), pushcarts, bicycles and literally thousands of pedestrians, the driver slowed down and pointed out a dark, poorly-lit entrance to a building where the upper floor windows were covered by closed shutters.

"This is opium den," the driver said, as he continued to slowly drive by the building he pointed out.

"Stop," said Jean. "That's where we want to go!"
Her partner on this adventure repeated the command, but the driver kept on moving down the street.

"Not safe for me to stop in front of place," the cab driver said. "Too dangerous. I will drive around the block and let you walk from the corner."

After finally manipulating his way around the block, avoiding small coal fires on the street where some people were cooking their food and others were arguing over the price of buying something, they were back to the street with the opium den's dark door. The driver stopped a long half-block from the den's entrance, took his payment and off he went in the old beater.

Jean and her friend walked along the crowded street until they reached the dim entryway to the opium den. They looked at one another and nodded their heads up and down. They opened the big, heavy wooden door and entered.

They maneuvered around inside the very darkened rooms lined with cubicles, usually seating two people who were puffing away on opium and oblivious to anyone around them. Jean called them "cages" as they wandered about in thick, noxious smoke. Some smokers appeared to be in a stupor caused by the drugs they were inhaling. Some were in a state of near-unconsciousness. Others were reacting to their drug intake by flying high and it wasn't on aviation octane.

Every so often, a little Thai man would approach the inquisitive pair and point toward an empty cage. The heads of both intruders shook back and forth, indicating "no" to the host. In some of the rooms there were eerie blue lights that hardly pierced the atmosphere. It was a strange place for strange people. And if you considered causing a commotion or disrupting the activities in the opium den, a couple of oversized giants would carry out the little Thai man's commands. He was the den's boss.

It wasn't long before the visiting pair departed the den. It was a crazy experience. After walking several blocks, Jean and her friend flagged down a cab and returned to the hotel for a nightcap. If they could have read the Thai language in local newspapers, they would have read about murders, almost on a nightly basis in Bangkok, and usually one in an opium den.

It was not unusual for Jean's Pan Am flight to touch down in any major European center. Paris, London, Frankfurt, Lisbon and Rome were frequented by the airline. Tehran, Iran; Karachi, Pakistan; New Delhi, India and Hong Kong, China were on Jean's Pan Am schedule, too. And as we've already mentioned, Jean's flights took her to the far reaches of Accra, Ghana; Johannesburg, South Africa and Kinshasa, Congo.

Jean was living in a world that was shrinking due to airplanes that could move passengers around the globe. This young Canadian woman was part of a history-making event that linked two continents together. It was the biggest advance in flight since Orville and Wilbur Wright got their "Flyer" off the ground at Kitty Hawk, North Carolina on December 17, 1903. Jean's inaugural flight certificate, signed by the president of Pan American Airlines, Juan Trippe on November 17, 1958 is a treasure that still hangs on the fly lady's wall.

"It was a thrill to be on that first jet plane to return across the Atlantic," said Jean. The first passenger jet flight in history to cross the Atlantic from New York to Paris was on October 26 of that year. Not long after, Jean was assigned to the return flight, bringing the speedy new bird, a Boeing 707, home from Europe at 600 miles per hour. Pan Am called the new plane the Intercontinental Jet Clipper. Being a stewardess on that history-making flight from London to New York was exciting for Jean. It marked a new age of flight – the Jet Age.

Jean was on the cutting edge of new flight travel around the world. The sleek Boeing 707s could carry 150 passengers and travel at speeds of 650 mph. The new jet cut the cockpit crew in half from six to three. What a difference from Pan Am's first transatlantic commercial passenger flight using a 41-ton "Dixie Clipper" that took off and landed on water. It was very much a flying boat, carrying 22 passengers and a crew of 12. This flight left Port Washington, Long Island in New York on June 28, 1939 with stops at Horta in the Azores, and Lisbon, Portugal before arriving at its destination – Marseilles, France on June 30, 1939.

Looking at her jet flight inaugural certificate, Jean chuckled. As she's aware, the British B.O.A.C. actually made it across the Atlantic three weeks before the Americans in a make-over jet Comet 4 aircraft from London to New York. She liked this one-upmanship by the British because of her family ties to Britain.

Another coup for the Canadian stewardess was knowing that the first international jet passenger flight was made in North America, when an Avro Canada jetliner took off from what was then called Malton Airport, now Toronto's Pearson International Airport, to land at the International Airport in New York City. This trip took place on April 18, 1950. The plane was carrying 15,000 airmail letters postmarked by an official Canadian imprint claiming to be the first mail carried by a jet aircraft. There were three crew and three passengers on board.

WALTER W. GOWING

CHAPTER SIXTEEN

IN LOVE!

The world began to look different for Jean Barrett. The flowers produced a sweeter fragrance; the birds' songs in the morning sounded like romantic ballads; the moon at night over the New York City skyline was bigger and brighter than ever before as Jean sensed romance in the air.

It was a hard decision to make: stay with Pan Am and continue the adventurous life she'd grown accustomed to, flying all over the world, or return to Toronto and marry a young doctor.

Indeed, the decision was hard for Jean. The world was her playground. She could often check her watch with the time on the face of Big Ben in London, England; have a drink at a sidewalk café in Istanbul, Turkey; take a cable car to the top of Table Mountain in Cape Town, South Africa; or hobnob with the world's elite over the Atlantic Ocean on a Pan Am flight. She had a choice to make and she made it. Love won.

It wasn't all without turbulence. There is one note of interruption to the love story, an air pocket of sorts. The bride-to-be almost didn't make it to the wedding.

On her way back to New York from an African trip,

Jean's flight had to land at Lajes Airport on the island of Terceira, one of the islands in the Azores. It is a group of nine islands, one of two autonomous regions of Portugal. The island grouping is found in the Atlantic Ocean, about 1,300 kilometres (800 miles) off the coast of Portugal. The islands are simply the peaks of underwater volcanic mountains that are subjected to earthquakes.

According to Jean, it might as well have been an earthquake holding her back from reaching home for her wedding. The plane had mechanical problems that would take a week to repair. The parts needed to repair the plane had to be brought from New York. There was no other flight off the island and the clock was ticking toward the moment when Jean would have to say, "I do."

Finally the aircraft was repaired and took off for New York. The next big thing for Jean was to hop a flight to Toronto. She arrived at the church just in time to marry Dr. Brian Fayle, a specialist in radiology, at Trinity College Chapel at the University of Toronto on September 1, 1961.

What about a honeymoon? It was back to New York for Jean and her new husband. They were off to London on a Pan Am flight that Jean previously served on as a stewardess. Brian said he'd be content to stay in London, but Jean had other places in the world to show him. They flew to Paris, Rome and then to Istanbul before returning home to Toronto.

After six years of galloping around the world on Pan

Am horsepower, Jean settled back into Canadian life. Today, the mother of four children lives in Cambridge, Ontario. One daughter, Daphne, lives in Toronto. Her three sons: Benjamin, Thomas and Jeffrey, all live in Vancouver, British Columbia.

Jean, I'm envious of all those flights that you made on Pan American World Airways. The places Pan Am took you on a world of adventure could only be a dream for most people. Lillian and I have been fortunate to visit many of the same places that you visited during your days in the air. We often took several flights, boats, even taxis, buses, camels or donkeys to reach our destinations. It was Pan Am that I wanted to fly on, but it retired its wings before I could climb aboard. Thank you for all of your memories that allow me to connect to such an amazing time in the air.

The epitaph for Pan American World Airways was written in 1991 when the last big bird in the sky returned to its nest, never to fly again with one of the finest flight crews to any airline ever assembled. It was a sad day when men and women stepped down to earth from their aircraft for the last time. The big "PA" logo would soon disappear.

Now, several decades since their last daily contact, more than 2,000 former stewards and stewardesses, including Jean, continue to be a close-knit group. Through 34 chapters in 20 countries, these former Pan Am employees are dedicated to raising funds and volunteering their time for charitable causes throughout the world.

The stewards and stewardesses of Pan Am formed World Wings International in 1959. They have continued to raise millions of dollars for worthwhile charities in a spirit of good stewardship. The organization CARE is a major recipient of funds raised by former Pan Am employees and their families known as World Wingers. They are now serving those unfortunate people in dire circumstances around the world. Pan Am is gone, but World Wingers are still a great crew.

Jean is shown above (far right) with her four sisters and her father, Thomas Barrett. Jean transitioned from registered nurse (below left) to the glamorous life of a Pan American Airways flight attendant (below right.)

After a flight to Accra, Ghana, the whole Pan Am flight crew was invited to a reception by Dr. Kwame Nkrumah, the first President of the free state of Ghana. Jean is pictured above, second from the left.

Jean receiving a miniature Freedom Bell from Willy Brandt in Berlin, 1960. At the time, Brandt was the mayor of Berlin.

Today, Jean (left) lives in Cambridge, Ontario and still recalls her days in the sky with the likes of Frank Sinatra, Rose Kennedy, Don DeFore, Zsa Zsa Gabor, Bing Crosby and Pat O'Brien

Below, Jean (on the right) dressed in her Pan Am uniform with a fellow stewardess.

WALTER W. GOWING

PART FIVE

DOWN UNDER

CHAPTER SEVENTEEN

DINNER IS SERVED

Another unusual world-class adventure that Lillian and I had in February and March of 2001 is a tale worth telling. We were frequent visitors to the island of Bermuda and often saw the dolphins training at Dolphin Quest. You can even swim with them at the facility. The organization educates the public through one-of-a-kind experiences and contributes millions of dollars in financial and in-kind support of conservation efforts. The scientific research turns into published works that continue to help researchers find solutions to the threats facing dolphins and whales worldwide.

A major training place for dolphins is in the South Pacific on the island of Moorea, part of the collection of Polynesian Islands. We decided to go there so I could write a travel piece on these wonderful creatures. It was part of a two-month trip to the South Pacific where I gathered lots of material for some exciting stories.

We packed our bags and set off from Toronto by air to Los Angeles where we checked into a comfortable hotel in time for dinner after a rather turbulent flight. The next night we departed L.A. for Papeete, Tahiti, arriving about 7:00 a.m. the next morning. A small van transferred us from the big international airport to a smaller domestic one about a kilometre away. With each of us wearing a garland of flowers around our neck, we boarded a small propeller-type plane operated by Air Moorea for a short flight, straight up and straight down. We passed over a narrow strip of blue ocean water that separated the islands and landed on a small runway in Moorea.

Our three-day stay at the Beachcomber Hotel, with its individual cottages hanging right out over the ocean waters, was like living in paradise. One evening the hotel staff set up about a dozen dinner tables in the bay, in water about a foot deep. They placed a shimmering white embroidered table cloth on each with a small lantern for light. They added tropical flowers in a beautiful ornate vase to decorate our table. After a tall glass of champagne and a few special canapés compliments of the chef, the five-course meal was every bit as fabulous as the fine English china it was plated on.

The waiters wore black tuxedos with fancy, frilly formal shirts and black bow ties. A satin stripe circled the jacket's collar with another satin stripe around the arm, just above the wrist. I should mention that their pants, with a satin stripe running down each leg, were cut off just below the knee. The tall waiters had the ocean water meeting the bottom half of their cut-offs. The short waiters had water lapping above their knees. They were all in bare feet, and for that matter, so were we.

This was something out of the ordinary, like a wacky Hollywood movie. But there were no lights or cameras, it was real life magic. Picture Lillian and I, among several other couples, just sitting there in the water eating dinner. French Polynesia is right in the middle of the Pacific Ocean. And there we were, sitting like islands as the water lapped against the table legs (and our legs, too) as the handsome Polynesian waiters dressed like penguins waded around us.

The longer we sat there, the higher the ocean water crept up our legs. The tide was slowly coming into the bay. We had about two hours to eat before the tide began to roll in and we had to abandon our table. It felt like we were on a sinking ship. We waded ashore and took up a relaxing position on comfortable lounge chairs to sit and listen to a small group of musicians play soothing south sea island music under the swaying palm trees. We watched as the tide continued to creep up the beach and flood the area where our dinner tables once stood. A night like this, you remember for a lifetime.

After getting my pictures and information on the dolphins over the next couple of days, we flew back to Papeete to spend a day before hopping on a midnight flight from Tahiti to Auckland, New Zealand. It was then over to Sydney, Australia for about four weeks travelling completely around the Down Under continent. My notebooks were full of stories and I took about 5,000 photographs to compliment my writing. Lillian kept a daily journal of our activities that always turns out to be extremely valuable when I'm back home and ready to write.

We visited Perth, a city on the west coast of Australia that Lillian considers to be in her top choices of cities worldwide. We've been there on a number of occasions. Leaving Perth, we flew north to Darwin, a remote frontier town. I love visiting Darwin, a city that still lives in its past. It is best to be there when it's free from cyclones. On one trip, Lillian and I arrived shortly after a cyclone hit and destroyed much of the city. In 2011, we arrived in Darwin just a couple days before a cyclone hit. We survived the storm of high winds, heavy rains, and an influx of crocodiles all over the place.

On our 2001 visit, we left by plane for the city of Cairns on Australia's east coast, an area known as the Gold Coast. Here we met up with our good friend Rob Bullas from Kitchener, Ontario, a short distance from our hometown of Cambridge. The rendezvous was prearranged, as Rob brought 30 people with him from Canada to tour the east coast of Australia and then hop over the explore New Zealand's North and South Islands, and then make a three-day stop on Fiji to top it off. Rob is a specialist on the South Pacific and has been to Australia about 50 times. Lillian and I planned to spend the next three weeks with Rob and his group.

Our mighty leader for these days of exploration had us ride on trains; ply the waters around the Great Barrier Reef in the Coral Sea; shoot across the sky in a gondola car, the Skyrail, high above the jungle-like rainforest of Queensland; and for some, climb the arches and walk across the Sydney Harbour Bridge. Transportation was sometimes by bus, train, boat or airplane, moving up and down the enchanting east coast of Australia.

CHAPTER EIGHTEEN

THE LOST GLACIER

After several days of trouping around Australia, Rob led us up the ramp to an aircraft that took us to the South Island of New Zealand. There, we boarded a sea-going ship to explore the fiords around Milford Sound and travelled by bus to see the glaciers. Lillian and I spent a few nights on a sheep ranch. There are more sheep in New Zealand than people. We visited one of the best natural museums that I have ever seen, located in Christchurch. Rob was ready to move us on to the North Island of New Zealand.

Early Sunday morning, March 18, 2001, all 33 of us took a half-hour drive out of the city to the Christchurch International Airport. I guess because it was a Sunday, traffic on the streets leading out of the city was very light. We headed out Fendalton Road that runs into Memorial Avenue, and before we knew it, we were at the airport.

Rob looked after checking our luggage while the group chatted about all of the unusual things we witnessed on the South Island of New Zealand. Unfortunately for the others, I was the only one to hike several miles to see the Fox Glacier. It was a long distance walk on very uneven and difficult terrain and the others decided that I should be the one to go looking for the glacier and report back. It made me feel like one of the early explorers: David Livingston who discovered Victoria Falls in the heart of Africa (whose statue I mimicked when Lillian and I travelled there); or Abel Janszoon Tasman finding the island he called Tasmania, south of Australia and then discovering New Zealand; or Christopher Columbus who discovered America.

I could see the glacier for a long distance. I thought I would never make it to the rim of the gigantic mound of ice. It was not unlike glaciers that I have seen in the Rocky Mountains of Canada or at the tip of South America. It was distinctive in a way that allowed me to walk along the clear, ice-cold creek that flowed from the melting glacier. As I approached this massive sheet of ice, I worried about its recession every year, a few inches due to climate change. In a few years, how much farther will my great-grandchildren have to walk to reach the melting giant?

Though the others on the Bullas-led trip felt it was too much of a physical trial to approach the glacier, I made it on foot. As I approached the crusty edge of ice, I reached in under its lip and gathered up some small pebbles of various colours from the glacier. There was a small breeze blowing down from the top of the glacier, and as the wind whipped around me, I hesitated for a moment. Was I hearing things? I thought the wind was saying to me, "Don't touch my property, it should remain with me forever."

It was frightening. I'm miles away from the rest of my party and it was getting later in the afternoon. The sun was now hiding behind some clouds.

Again, there was a voice in the wind that I believed was telling me that I was trespassing on an ancient glacier. A burial ground for who knows what? Could it be land where dinosaurs roamed and the wild-tusked beasts that were bigger than today's elephants lived and died?

"There are strange things done in the midnight sun..." and more of Robert Service's poem of The Cremation of Sam McGee was running through my head like an old suspense drama on the radio.

More of the poem kept coming back to me as I walked faster, stumbled and ran, for I had hours to go with the glacier at my back and dusk beginning to hover above me.

"Yet, taint being dead, it's my awful dread of the icy grave that pains..." from the pen of the poet, frightening me as I covered twice as much distance going down the slope in half the time as I did climbing toward the giant frozen mass earlier.

Robert Service is one of my favourite poets. This Canadian produced ballads that could stir your blood about the cold north frontier and the Yukon territory. His words seemed right at home at this desolate spot, miles from any living soul in New Zealand. The only companion I had at this moment was Robert Service, his chilling words running through my head. With a few pebbles rattling in my pocket, I fled the scene of the talking winds and glacier spouting its water from cold, jagged lips.

The thought struck me, what if it were a dark, cloudy night without moon or stars and I couldn't find my way back. I thought I'd better hurry.

Finally, there before me in the distance was a wooden area where the path I had taken up the mountainside stood out like a welcome mat. Although I was somewhat winded, I increased my speed, climbing several feet up the wooded slope until I reached the clearing at the top. There, waiting for me, was Lillian and the rest of the gang. They gave out a cheer and Rob packed us all onto the bus and headed for our night's stay.

CHAPTER NINETEEN

WELCOME, PRIME MINISTER

Back at the Christchurch International Airport, a new page was about to be turned. Another story was about to begin.

For me, the whole adventure around Australia and New Zealand climaxed with the events that were about to take place over the next few hours. This might be one of my favourite stories of all time.

Like a good shepherd keeping his sheep, Rob Bullas got everyone in line and without a sheepdog or a shepherd's crook, ushered us out through the door and across the tarmac to the waiting plane. Naturally, everything in New Zealand is best illustrated by using sheep. As I mentioned before, the sheep outnumber the people. It's nearly 12 sheep for every human.

As our luggage was being loaded on at the front of the aircraft just behind the cockpit compartment, passengers climbed several steps up a portable ramp at the rear of the plane to board. Rob was first up the stairs, ducking his head of white curly hair as he entered the aircraft. He selected the rear seat on the right-hand side of the aisle. He exchanged greetings with the stewardess just inside the aircraft and mentioned that his flock was following behind him. One by one, we ducked our heads as we entered the plane and the charming stewardess welcomed us on board and let us know that it was open seating and we could sit wherever we wanted. There was one centre aisle with two seats on either side that made up the configuration. It was a 48-seat passenger airplane but about a dozen seats were empty when we were ready to leave Christchurch for Rotorua.

It appeared that everyone was on board when a well-dressed man in a black suit and wearing sunglasses walked up the aisle to the front of the plane where a stewardess was standing. I particularly noticed this fellow because he looked like an undercover CIA or FBI type of character. In our travels all around the world, these guys all look alike. They must all drink the same water or beer and have the same tailor and barber. The stewardess and the cloak-and-dagger character concluded their animated conversation and then he retreated back down the aisle and out the door.

The stewardess made her move. She walked from front to back, stopping next to Rob in the rear seat. Another conversation took place and then the flight attendant disappeared out the door. Something mysterious was going on and I was about to get up and go back to speak with Rob when the other stewardess appeared at the back door for another short conversation with Rob. I decided to sit tight and just observe the strange happenings.

Finally, one of the stewardesses went to the front of the aircraft, followed by one of the dark-suited men who was still wearing sunglasses (that were really not needed on the plane). Then a new person appeared on the scene dressed in black slacks with a long black dress top and a greenish coloured jacket. She strode up the aisle, her long legs covering giant steps with her briefcase out in front like the bow of a ship cutting through the water. Right behind her, trying to keep up was another lookalike CIA type in his uniform black suit and sunglasses. The woman took the second seat from the front. The first bodyguard, if you could call him that, took a seat in the front row and the second mystery man took a seat in the row behind the unknown woman. The drama of it all went unnoticed by the other passengers on board.

The two propeller engines projecting from the lengthy wing stretching across the top of the Air New Zealand flight's cabin began to roar and the plane started to move down the runway. In moments we were off the ground, making a half circle in the air and heading to Rotorua. It was a normal flight with a light lunch served. Before we knew it, the pilot was announcing that we should remain in our seats, fasten our seatbelts and prepare to land. Over the PA system, one of the flight attendants thanked us for flying Air New Zealand.

Once the plane came to a complete stop on the ground, Rob was the first one up and out the door, heading down the stairs to the terminal. He told me later that he took the seat at the rear of the plane because he can get into the terminal quickly to check out the number of taxis available and get a van for the luggage. He made a call from Christchurch to have the vehicles waiting for us, but that doesn't always happen as planned. See? He's an expert at this stuff.

He said the stewardesses were concerned about his comfort sitting in the back seat, as it had less legroom and thought that he might be happier sitting in one of the open seats near the front of the plane. He insisted that he was satisfied with his chosen seat, unaware that someone else wanted the rear seat to be the first one off the plane in Rotorua.

My curiosity was far too great to let all the mysterious movements and people on the plane pass by without finding out what was going on. What were the security people doing on the plane? Who was that woman? As Lillian and I left the aircraft, I noticed that the three unknown people at the front of the plane hadn't moved. They were still sitting there when we left the plane and descended the stairway to the ground below. It was only a few steps to the terminal building and we entered a door with a sign that read "Arrivals."

Just inside the door stood four men dressed in various coloured suits. I think two were wearing blue shirts, one man had a white shirt on, and the fourth's shirt had all the colours of the rainbow. Being a journalist, you have to be observant of the most precise, trivial and petty details when building a story. You need the facts, all the facts.

I quickly turned to Lillian and said for her to go ahead to look after our luggage. Something was up and I had to stay and find out what it was. These guys looked like the mayor and city councillors, if I had to guess. Three of them were wearing ties, and the fourth (with the rainbow shirt) had his shirt open at the neck.

Everyone's attention was suddenly focused on the arrival door. One of those black-suited protectors wearing sunglasses opened the door and held it open for the lady in black with the green jacket to enter. The four suspected dignitaries that were waiting in line went to attention. I quickly lined up with them, making me number five. I always dress a certain way to travel, especially by air. I was wearing my dark blue jacket with the dual vents, white shirt, my red and blue striped tie with my grey pants. I always had polished black leather shoes. (Charlie Stager, former clerk-treasurer of the County of Waterloo once told me that whenever you are interviewing anyone, always look at the person's shoes. He said it tells a great deal about the person. If they don't bother to keep their shoes clean and polished, how do they keep their desk, their room and their work?).

The mystery woman approached the first man in line.

"Welcome, Prime Minister," he said, extending his hand to the woman, who shook it briefly.

"Welcome, Prime Minister," the second man said, following suit with the extension of his hand and a quick shake by the woman.

"Welcome, Prime Minister," said the third, the one with the wild rainbow shirt. He too reached out and quickly shook the hand of the lady whom I presumed by now to be the prime minister.

"Welcome, Prime Minister," said the fourth man. He also shared a quick handshake with the woman.

This important dignitary, very tall for a woman with dark, short straight hair, stepped in front of me. She wore a fine gold chain around her neck with a small blue opal that hung just below the top cut of her neckline. The jewelry was not outlandish or extraordinary, just a touch of class. Why am I taking notice of all of this when I have to say something? The wheels inside my head were spinning in an attempt to come up with something brilliant to say to this very important woman. And what did I say?

"Welcome, Prime Minister."

What an original line. I said exactly what the others said ahead of me.

"Welcome," I repeated, as I extended my hand towards her.

Her face lit up with a big smile that stretched nearly from ear to ear. This was the first time that I noticed a smile on her face. It made her look much more attractive. As I extended my right arm, she took my hand and squeezed it. She didn't let go. I'm sure everyone in the terminal was staring at us. The four men ahead of me, obviously representing the municipality or something of similar importance in that part of the country, stood there looking puzzled about what was happening. I'm sure they were asking themselves who this guy was at the end of the line.

"You're Canadian," said Prime Minister Helen Clark.

"How do you know?" I replied.

"Your accent," she said. "It gives you away. We all have an accent when we are away from home."

"How did you know I was Canadian?" I asked, puzzled.

"My husband spent a year lecturing at the University of Toronto and I spent quite some time there too," said the very friendly lady as she finally released my right hand.

"My name is Walter Gowing and I'm a writer and journalist from Cambridge, Ontario, just west of Toronto," I informed her. "I'm very honoured to meet you, Prime Minister."

"It has been my pleasure," said Prime Minister Clark.

"Would you have time for a short interview?" I asked, pushing my luck a little further. "I would really appreciate the opportunity to ask you a few questions."

The two bodyguards in their sunglasses were stewing about, trying to get her attention. One finally approached her and informed her that time was of the essence and the cars were waiting outside the terminal.

She turned to me and said, "Give me a moment to freshen up, Walter, and then we will talk."
Off she went to the second floor VIP washroom. The four official representatives chosen to welcome the prime minister stood talking to one another in a low whisper. They glanced at me a number of times and I

smiled back.

As I waited for the Prime Minister of New Zealand to return, I noticed the two security guards who had accompanied her on the plane nervously standing together, a few feet away from anyone else. They looked like they had lost something, like say, a prime minister. There they stood, looking around the airport reception room, whispering something to one another every few minutes. Really, it seemed pretty safe to be the Prime Minister of New Zealand.

Back in Canada at this time, the prime minister for nearly a decade was always surrounded by a platoon of Royal Canadian Mounted Police. The Mounties traded in their bright red jackets and black breeches for dark suits and dark glasses. They parked their faithful horses in the stables while playing bodyguard to Mr. Harper. The plainclothes cops thoroughly checked out everything ahead of the PM's movements in Canada.

At the Rotorua Airport, Prime Minister Clark had just ventured off to the restroom by herself. No checking out things ahead of time. No extra security needed for her to freshen up and make a pit stop. I often wondered if the Canadian guardians of the prime minister were checking to see if the seat was up or down before he was allowed to enter the washrooms?

Before long, Prime Minister Clark returned to where I was waiting. I asked numerous questions, how was the current political climate? "Hot." She was very open with her answers, including that she was very proud of the All Blacks (the nation's rugby team). She added some of her own questions and remarks to the mix.

I thought her two assistants were going to go crazy while the cavalcade of cars outside sat idling in anticipation of her appearance at any moment.

"I really must go now," she said. "I think the others are getting worried about the time. I'm to make a speech and cut a ribbon to officially open the revamped Rotorua International Stadium."

As the prime minister walked out of the airport, she turned to me and said, "It was nice meeting you, Walter. Bye now."

I followed her outside and watched as the dark-suited pair with the sunglasses ushered her safely inside a shiny black limousine and as the car moved away from the curb, I raised my camera to take a picture. Through my viewfinder, I saw Mrs. Clark tap the driver on the shoulder and the car stopped. The window in the backseat came down and the Prime Minister leaned out a little bit and shouted to me, "Is this better?"

I took my picture, she waved and I waved back. Off the car went down the road. As I stood there watching the automobile disappear in the distance, I felt that I was almost in a daze over the events of the last few minutes. What a wonderful opportunity I had, meeting a world leader who was so pleasant and kind to me.

I think our former prime minister in Canada, Stephen Harper, was allergic to journalists. He avoided the media as much as he could, most of his news clips were staged by party peons. (Remember former media people that Harper appointed to the senate like Mike Duffy and Pamela Wallin?)

It was invigorating for a journalist to meet a person like Prime Minister Clark, who sincerely took time out of her very limited amount to be honest and open in our conversation.

Helen Clark was the 37th Prime Minister of New Zealand and served three consecutive terms from 1999 to 2008. She was selected in 2009 by world countries to become the Administrator of the United Nations Development Program. She was sworn in by UN Secretary-General Ban Ki-Moon as the first woman to lead this program. Forbes magazine placed Clark as the 61st most powerful woman in the world.

After Prime Minister Clark was out of sight at the airport at Rotorua, I turned to walk over to where our party had gathered with Rob Bullas and Lillian. The group was watching the entire interaction between the unknown mystery woman and me. They were very curious.

"Who was that woman?" asked Rob.

"Walter did you know that woman from some place?" Lillian chirped.

I replied to both of them by saying that I didn't know her before today, but now we were the best of friends.

"Who is she?" they said in unison, like a duet.

"Only the Prime Minister of New Zealand, Helen Clark," I answered.

She was the mysterious lady on the plane that a fellow from Kitchener wouldn't give up his seat so that she could sit at the back. Rob's face turned bright red. He said he was embarrassed that he'd taken the seat the prime minister wanted. The poor guy didn't know who the seat was for when the flight attendant asked him if he'd like to relocate to the front, and he'd declined her offer.

"I had no idea they wanted the seat for the prime minister," Rob said, looking like a little boy who had just spilled a bowl of sugar all over the kitchen floor.

"I would have gladly given up my seat if only they had told me Mrs. Clark wanted to sit at the back," he continued. "I'm kind of choked up."

Rob, the loveable big guy, would give you the shirt off his back if you needed it.

"Gosh," he stammered. "What if they don't let me back in the country again? I hope I didn't offend the prime minister."

After our stay in Rotorua, we motored up to Auckland for our last leg of the New Zealand journey. We stopped along the way at the Waitomo Glow Worm Caves. Inside the caves is a place that looks like a giant cathedral with excellent acoustics. We sang 'O Canada!'

at the top of our lungs. Lillian sang a part of it in French.

After a couple of days in Auckland, we ventured to the airport to fly onwards to Fiji. As we gathered around Rob in the departure lounge waiting for our flight to be called, we wanted to know if we should check out the passenger list. There might be a president or some other type of dignitary onboard with us and we didn't want Rob to be embarrassed again. Of course, we all laughed (including Rob). The great thing about Rob Bullas is that he has a fantastic sense of humour. Lillian and I would travel anywhere in the world with him.

If Rob said, "Fly with me," I surely would.

CHAPTER TWENTY

RECIPE SWAP

While I was meeting with Prime Minister Helen Clark at the Rotorua Airport, Rob Bullas was organizing luggage and transportation to our local accommodation, the Novotel Hotel. The King of Thailand purchased this hotel as a gift for his daughter.

"I must meet that king sometime and perhaps he would buy me the Shangri-La Fijian Resort in Fiji," Rob and his great sense of humour joked. We were all to spend a few days there after we left New Zealand.

The Novotel Hotel has a wonderful spa with highly-trained registered Maori massage therapists who do excellent work. To complement the massage, you can bath in a choice of mineral water or pure spring water, both are a real treat for the body.

As usual, Lillian and I had an agenda of our own. The two of us visited Rotorua Primary School where we had the privilege of meeting local teacher Kim Delamere and her class of 29 students, all ages nine or 10. About half the students were Maori. Lillian joined Kim in teaching some mathematics and spelling lessons. These are the special experiences one can enjoy away from the normal tourist attractions.

When Rob heard about what a great time we had at the school, he said he was sorry to have missed it, as he could use a little "more education." We reminded him that the three of us had visited a French Polynesian primary school on the island of Bora Bora back in 2001. We were on a cruise around the Pacific Islands that included Moorea and Papeete. A few years later, Lillian and I returned to these beautiful islands.

I must complete the story of New Zealand's Prime Minister Clark, actually the story of the Prime Minister's husband Peter Davis. At the time, Peter was a professor at Otago University's School of Medicine.

I did a number of major stories on the prime minister and one in particular on the treatment her husband was receiving from the media. Newspapers carried these stories back in Canada.

Here is the entire story with its five-column headline under my by-line "WALTER GOWING Speaks Out":

New Zealand OM defends spouse from 'scumbags'

My brief encounter recently with New Zealand Prime Minister Helen Clark was indeed very pleasant.

We were both passengers on the same Air New Zealand flight from Christchurch to Rotorua. After landing in Rotorua, a north island city with a high population of Maori people, we had a few moments to chat before she was whisked off to a public ribbon-cutting ceremony.

When there is the smell of a scandal, the media can be merciless. During the previous week in New Zealand, the prime minister's husband Peter Davis, a professor of public health at Otago University's School of Medicine in Christchurch, had been under fire for routing e-mails through the prime minister's office.

The e-mail in question was directed to the Health Research Council and recommended a Canadian professor to conduct a review of New Zealand's drug-funding agency, Pharmac.

The grant was awarded to a team from Otago University that included Doctor Joel Lexchin of Toronto. Professor Davis had forwarded Doctor Lexchin's curriculum vitae to Health Minister Annette King's office via his wife's office.

Professor Davis was accused of using his wife's office so that the application for funding would take on the appearance of being sanctioned by the prime minister.

Doctor Lexchin was appointed to head the review and was paid $5,000 Canadian dollars for about 10 days work in New Zealand. In addition to the money, the contract called for his return business-class air ticket from Toronto to Auckland to be paid for by the health authority.

Although a couple of New Zealanders were interested in the short-term position, Doctor Lexchin had the best qualifications for the job. The Canadian professor even warned Syd Bradley, chairman of the Health Funding Authority, that he was a friend of Professor Davis and that he personally knew Prime Minister Clark. He wanted everything up front and in the open.

This whole thing started when Health Minister King asked Professor Davis for suggestions, as the HFA was looking for someone to take on the review of Pharmac. Professor Davis sent the name of the Canadian professor by e-mail to his wife's office and requested that it be forwarded on to the health authority. It was a simple thing to do because he knew his wife's e-mail address and not the one for the health authority. So what's the problem?

Well, politicians in opposition to the prime minister jumped up and down in the chambers of parliament and accused Ms. Clark of using her office on behalf of her husband to give a contract to a friend. Some of the media went wild with this story as though the PM had sold the country to the Australians, their bitter rivals in football and other things. One columnist compared the situation to that of Caesar, dating back more than 2,00 years. He used the immortal phrase, "Caesar's wife must be above suspicion."

Another columnist revealed that while Prime Minister Clark is busy in parliament, her husband is home doing the housework. He is accused also of cooking up some exotic meals for his wife. Well, a lot of women would want a man like that around the house.

While politicians and the media took some delight in attacking the PM's husband, Ms. Clark came back with both guns smoking. She defended her husband, saying that he "had an impeccable 31-year career as a researcher."

She let the opposition know that they were "scumbags"and "sleaze-balls."

"I just regret that the petty, filthy nature of politics in this country subjects someone to this sort of scurrilous attack, which is designed to impugn that professional reputation simply because they have the fortune, or misfortune, to be married to a woman who is the prime minister."

Go get them, Helen. I'm on your side! But Madam Prime Minister, don't be surprised if I tell you that back in Canada we have the same kind of antics going on in our legislatures and parliament too.

I agree with you that families sometimes pay a very high price for the political career of a parent or spouse. Politicians are legitimate targets but families are not.

Oh, by the way Helen, I'd like to swap some recipes with Peter sometime.

WALTER W. GOWING

CHAPTER TWENTY-ONE

THE CHEF

This story is just too precious to leave out of any book wherein Rob Bullas is included. On one particular trip south, we didn't exactly make it all the way to what is considered 'Down Under'. This time we made it to Hawaii and visited some of the eight larger islands but bypassed the 124 smaller ones.

Known as the Aloha State, we visited the islands of Oahu, Kauai, Maui and the big island of Hawaii. As there is more water than land in this area of the Pacific Ocean, we visited the islands by ship.

Hawaii is located north of the equator, about the same distance north as Baja California. After visiting Hawaii, we headed south and crossed the equator, making our way Down Under.

This time our destination was not kangaroo country, but the French Provincial Islands east of northern Australia. We explored the islands of Tahiti, Bora Bora and Moorea.

It is really an episode that happened at the beginning of this whole adventure that I want to tell you about. If I described the whole trip and the unexpected funny things that happened, it would become another book.

I guess it all started when Lillian and I flew into Honolulu on the island of Oahu. That is the same island where you find Pearl Harbor, and who can forget the surprise Japanese attack on the United States naval base there on December 7, 1941. That is the day the United States joined the Allies to fight the evil Axis Powers in the Second World War.

As customary on these islands, we had leis placed around our necks when we disembarked the aircraft. A car was waiting at the airport to take us straight to the Prince Hotel in Honolulu. It was late in the evening, so after check-in, we went to our room and it wasn't long before we were both asleep.

We arrived in Honolulu a few days before we were to meet up with our Bullas group because we wanted to take an island-hopping cruise in the Pacific. Lillian and I had been there before and it was nice to revisit some of the same spots – the Sheraton Hotel and Waikiki Beach. Lillian still laughs at me when anyone mentions hula dancing.

One evening we were walking along the beach when a native group of dancers dragged me in for a lesson in hula. I told Lillian that she shouldn't laugh at me because I was pretty good at the hula. It must be my white hair because I've been pulled out of crowds in China, New Zealand and Thailand to dance with some very beautiful girls.

We were enjoying the luxury of the Prince Hotel with the hundreds of small watercraft right on its doorstep.

The sailing vessels had their masts all pointing skyward like school children in a classroom, all with their hands up and ready to answer the teacher's questions. There were great views from our hotel room overlooking the oceanfront marina and an extended view of the blue waters of the Pacific Ocean. Lillian particularly loved the eloquence of the Prince's lobby with its giant white pillars and its marble flooring. Colourful carpets were spread around the floor where comfortable chairs invited you to sit and enjoy.

On the day we were scheduled to meet Rob Bullas, who was bringing 21 travelers from Toronto to Honolulu for a cruise, we met him in the lobby. After a hug and kiss for Lillian and a handshake with me, we sat down in the lobby and talked for a while.

"Oh," said Rob. "I want you to meet a really interesting guy."

As you may have gathered from earlier chapters, I'm always game to meet interesting people. Rob escorted us across the lobby where we found 87-year-old Arthur Bamford sitting. This Kitchener man once headed Waterloo Region's biggest electrical contracting company.

Art told us he was born in Hamilton on February 28, 1915. After graduating from Hamilton Tech, he worked for General Electric. His father George came from England and his mother Ellen was from Toronto. He had two sisters and Art's income helped the family through some lean times. His father had epilepsy and at times couldn't work at his tire repair shop.

In 1940, Art married Vivian, a co-worker at GE. They had a son Robert, who taught at Conestoga College and a daughter Barbara, who lived in Grimsby.

During the Second World War, Art served in the Royal Canadian Air Force specializing in radar. He was posted to radar engineering headquarters in Ottawa after training at Clinton radar base and the University of Guelph. At the end of the war he left the service with the rank of a flying officer.

Returning to GE in Hamilton as a salesman, he developed a big account with Sutherland-Schultz in Kitchener. In 1947, Ed Schultz visited Art to join the company. It wasn't long before Art was running the company.

In 1950, Art and his two partners, Bob Pugsley and Steve Manich, bought the company. Business boomed as Ontario changed to 60 cycles and thousands of 25-cycle motors were rewound.

Business didn't keep Art from taking part in community affairs. He was president of the Kitchener Chamber of Commerce, president of the Kitchener Kiwanis Club and president of the Freeport Hospital board.

Art loved curling, golfing and travelling. He's been just about everywhere in the world, he could really give Lillian and our passports a run for their money, though Art said it's not as enjoyable travelling alone since his wife died. For many years, Art and Vivian were good friends with Rob's parents, Roy and Ruth Bullas. Art explained that after this trip, the one country he'd still like to visit is Russia. He wanted to see what those "Reds" are up to over there.

It was getting close to dinnertime and Rob suggested we all go over to the Outrigger Hotel a few blocks away for what he said would be a great dining experience. Rob gathered up a few more of his travelling group and we hopped into taxis and were off on another adventure in search of a good meal.

The dining room at the Outrigger Hotel was located right on the shoreline with the waves washing up against the building. Lillian and I sat at a table with our new acquaintance, Art. We were all served drinks and Art had a second before we finished our first. He was a great conversationalist.

Art could be unintentionally funny. We were having a wonderful time chatting with this senior citizen who looked at the world like he was still 20 years old. The waitress took our dinner order and soon returned with our appetizers. Rob stopped by to make sure everything was going well. The evening was very enjoyable so far.

I think maybe I spoke too soon about how things were going. The waiter showed up with our main course. It was a special salad plate for Lillian featuring fruits and vegetables of every colour in the rainbow. Art received the fish, and I got my steak.

In Hawaii the native people are accustomed to volcanoes erupting and hot lava bubbling up and over the rim to run down the side of the mountain and into the sea. Just for one moment I thought that's what happened at our table.

"My God," exploded Art, staring at his dinner in front of him. What was going on?

"These stupid idiots forgot to cook my fish," he yelled.

He had ordered Mahi Mahi, a favourite Hawaiian fish dish.

"It's not cooked," bellowed Art. "It's raw. Hell, I'm not eating raw fish. Get the waiter back over here."

He held up the plate for everyone to see, and sure enough, it hadn't been cooked.

When Art complained to the waiter that his Mahi Mahi was "uncooked" and asked him how he expected anyone to eat uncooked fish, the waiter just smiled.

"You see, sir," the kind waiter said. "People cook their own fish or steaks here."

Pointing to the other side of the room, the waiter noted a giant barbecue across the dining area where patrons cook their own food. It was even a surprise to me, but I have been to other restaurants where this takes place.

"Damn," said Art. "I'm on vacation and I'm not doing the cooking."

This is where Chef Walter jumped in to save the meal. I quickly volunteered to cook the fish (and my steak, too). I put on an apron that was a little too large, as it hung from my neck to my ankles. That wasn't going to change the taste of the fish. There I was, decked out in my long white apron, slaving over a hot barbecue in the dining room of the Outrigger Hotel in Honolulu. I even had requests from other patrons asking me if I would cook their dinners too. I delivered the fish and the steak back to our table and I must say, Art really enjoyed his Mahi Mahi. Art left a good tip for the poor waiter who had taken some rather strong language from the older gentleman about the raw fish.

As we left the dining room I thought to myself, I had to cook dinner but thank goodness I didn't have to wash the dishes!

Rob Bullas, president of Bullas Travel in Kitchener, Ontario has led different tour groups to Australia over 50 times.

Rumour has it Rob knows every kangaroo on the continent by name.

The majestic Fox Glacier on the South Island of New Zealand.

The eerie winds whipping around the ice are like whispers to a lone traveller.

FLY WITH ME

Top – My wife Lillian in the infinity pool at our hotel in the South Pacific.

Bottom left – New Zealand Prime Minister Helen Clark arriving at the Rotorua airport.

Bottom right – A fellow world traveller, Art Bamford

WALTER W. GOWING

AFTERWORD

In retrospect, "Fly With Me" provided an outlet to tell the great, comical and wild adventures that my wife Lillian and I have been privileged to undertake in this beautiful and wonderful world we live in. People and places around the globe make for a homogeneous mosaic that keeps the planet spinning.

As we look back through the pages of "Fly With Me" I think of Happy Harry, the little penguin who bonded with me in Patagonia. I sometimes go to sleep at night, thinking about this little friend dressed in his cute black and white tuxedo.

The daredevil in me overtook common sense when I volunteered to ride an ostrich in South Africa. This flightless bird could run faster than my father's 1936 Oldsmobile. And I can't forget the Indian Pacific train ride across Australia, when I helped the train manager and engineer chase sleeping camels off the railway track.

It was a real pleasure to get to know Jean Fayle and hear about her flights across the Atlantic to exotic destinations. Years later, I had the opportunity to visit many of the same places where Jean touched down while flying with Pan American Airways. And how about the wow factor on the night we ate dinner in the waters of the Pacific Ocean? And no, I wasn't going to say the wow-factor in one of the Australian outback's saloons...

One of life's most enchanting moments was when the tide rolled into that French Polynesian lagoon while we sat eating delicacies on fine china, the tuxedoed waiters up to their knees in the surf.

I will never forget the angry glacier on New Zealand's South Island where I pocketed a handful of tiny pebbles from under its lip. The wild talking winds driving me away, as if I were facing certain doom.

It was a rare occasion when a Canadian journalist interviewed the same country's prime minister. Meeting Prime Minister Helen Clark in an impromptu line up in Rotorua's airport was fantastic.

It took many air miles to cover the various territories in this book. "Fly With Me" brings us together and allows you to experience the adventures from your favourite reading spot, whether it's in your living room or on a plane (train, bus or boat) to a wild destination of your own. I hope you "Fly With Me" again.

ABOUT THE AUTHOR

Standing his ground in front of a charging elephant, a close encounter with a ferocious lion or being attacked by a crazed monkey is all part of getting the story to this journalist and author of adventure.

Walter Gowing and his wife Lillian have travelled to more than 100 countries around the globe and spent a total of one year at sea during a 10 year period, all in the name of finding exciting news and adventure stories for his readers.

Although his weekly newspaper column in the *Cambridge Times* covers events and happenings in and around the community of Cambridge, Ontario, Canada, his books reach to far off places in Asia, Africa and South America. The normally mild-mannered columnist becomes a risk taker when in the jungles of Africa or on the border of Yemen and Saudi Arabia. Gowing's life has been packed with excitement, danger and intrigue.

For the author, sometimes the most rewarding experiences are the ones he doesn't need a passport for – at home in Cambridge. His work in the community earned him numerous awards for community service. In 1999 he received the Bernice Adams Special Trustee Award from the city, the Queen Elizabeth Golden Jubilee Medal in 2002; and was honoured for his lifetime commitment to community service with an induction into the Preston High School Hall of Fame in 2007.

In 2014, the Galt-Cambridge Lions Club presented him

with the prestigious Melvin Jones Fellow Award for dedicated humanitarian services on behalf of the Lions Clubs International Foundation. Gowing is one of the few non-members of the club to receive this honour.

Gowing has been involved in minor hockey since the first time he laced his skates at the age of five. A former president of the Preston Boys' Hockey Association, he has been a board member of the Preston International Hockey Tournament for more than half a century.

The author was Chief Librarian of Waterloo County for 12 years, Executive Director of the Midwestern Regional Development Council, Executive Secretary of the Niagara Escarpment Commission, Chief Administrator of Niagara Escarpment Public Hearings and Deputy Director of Information for the Ministry of Natural Resources at Queen's Park in Toronto. He also served 15 years as a board member of Curriculum Services Canada.

Gowing has been a magazine editor and journalist covering stories in Moscow, London, Copenhagen and Darwin (Australia) for major newspapers. His love for adventure is reflected in his books.